11 Global Leaders
WOI

MW01291432

With Real-Life Success Lessons and Take-Aways

Nidhi Agarwal

INDIA • SINGAPORE • MALAYSIA

Notion Press Media Pvt Ltd

No. 50, Chettiyar Agaram Main Road,
Vanagaram, Chennai, Tamil Nadu – 600 095

First Published by Notion Press 2021
Copyright © Nidhi Agarwal 2021
All Rights Reserved.

ISBN 978-1-63997-678-2

Contents

Preface to the Book

Hello, thanks for buying this book.

Let me start as to why I wrote this book. I am an avid reader, and as a financial professional, I couldn't find a single book that covers stories of women Chief Financial Officers (CFOs)! Because of the pandemic in the year 2020, I had a lot of free time during weekends, and that's when I thought about telling the stories of some of the incredible women across the globe who have made it to the top in the finance world. I started working on this book in 2020 by reaching out to women leaders around the world. I was a bit sceptical if I could connect with them at a deeply personal level, given their diverse cultures and backgrounds. To my surprise and delight, each of the ladies covered in the book welcomed me into their life journeys with great warmth.

I have enjoyed writing this book. I feel a sense of obligation to the women who have entrusted me with their stories. I want every young girl to dream and aspire by reading these stories. I hope this book will inspire many women finance professionals to break the glass ceiling and aim to become CFOs one day!!

As per the Year 2018 McKinsey report, males and females in finance start their careers on equal footing. As they go up the ladder, women account for only 19% of the positions of power. Also, a recent study by Catalyst shows that less than 13% of the women in Finance make it to leadership roles like CFO. Further, a study by Harvard Business Review mentions that most women leave the workforce partly because they don't have female role models at the top in the finance world. I hope that by reading this book, women can visualize their role models and get inspired. I have been lucky that early in my career, I got to work with Kristina Isherwood, who was my role model, and her story on "*A true fighter who never gives up*" is covered in this book.

In my book, I would say that the stories are not glamorous stories of women with superpowers saving the earth from alien attacks. But these are real stories of ordinary women who reached some of the topmost positions in the finance world with their resilience and belief that an individual is an amalgamation of humans around them. You will realize that careers are not built in a vacuum but rather by a network of people supporting you and challenging you to be the best version of yourself. Family, friends, colleagues, leaders, mentors, and teams are part of that network. This network helped and challenged them to grow and develop beyond what they could have imagined for themself.

You will find that many women leaders in this book didn't have the best resources in childhood. Yet, they navigated their way to climb up the corporate ladder in big global companies. Each of them strongly hopes that if they can inspire even a few women with their life stories, it would be an outstanding achievement.

As I interacted with the women leaders covered in this book and dug deeper into their stories for insights, below were some of my learnings were as below:

1. There is no substitute for hard work. Each story in the book would demonstrate how each woman leader has worked hard to earn her position and sustain it. None of them took success for granted, and they prove themselves each day.

2. You should be passionate about your work. As you climb up the corporate ladder, the working hours would increase; unless you enjoy what you are doing, you won't be able to cope.

3. It is crucial to choose the right life partner and build (Yes, 'build') a support system at home. Share your dreams with your family and leaders at work to find sponsors.

4. Stay humble. Humility is a hallmark of success. The women leaders in this book have detached their designations or work titles from what they are as human beings. Humility is the foundation of being ambitious!!

5. Building relationships and networking at the workplace is critical. In a world where investors don't want to be surprised, it is vital that the CFO of the company is well connected at all levels in the company.

6. Influence people to achieve change instead of directing change. In times of uncertainty, dialogue with team members and hearing diverse perspectives is critical for decision making.

7. Constant self-evaluation and having insatiable curiosity are essential. You must constantly upgrade yourself and keep pushing yourself outside the comfort zone if you want to grow.

Each person's circumstances are different, and your story can't be the same as anyone else's. By reading this book, I hope every woman can understand that Ambition, Humility, Profession, and prosperous family life can all co-exist!!

I would like to thank my LinkedIn network, Purvi Tantia, Dr. Niru Kumar, Nalin Chandana, Monica Saxena, and Pawan Tayla, for connecting me to some of the fantastic women leaders covered in this book.

Thanks to Shruti Sapra, Shruti Tantia, the Notion Press team, my husband Mohit Agarwal and my son, Darsh Agarwal, who helped me edit the book.

I also want to thank all the great leaders I have worked with to date; they always motivate me and challenge me to keep raising the bar.

At last, a big thanks to my parents Pawan Bholusaria and Madhu Bholusaria, who gave me wings to fly and the courage to dream big, my in-laws late MBL Agarwal and Pushplata Agarwal, along with my husband Mohit, who have always supported my professional dreams. My siblings Shikha and Nitin and my sisters-in-law Parul and Nupur, for always being there beside me.

You will be happy to know that this book's net proceeds will be donated to non-profit organizations in India working towards women's education and empowerment.

Disclaimers:

The views, thoughts, and opinions expressed in the book belong solely to the author and are not necessarily of the author's employer(s), organization(s), committee(s), or other groups or individuals. The author has written this book personally and does not represent any of her employers, either past or present.

The author has made every effort to ensure that the information in this book was correct at press time. The book is not intended to hurt the sentiments of any individual, custom, country, brand, institution, company, or corporation. The author and the women leaders covered in the book do not assume and hereby disclaim any liability to any party for any loss, damage or disruption caused by errors or omissions, whether such errors or omissions result from negligence, accident, or any other cause.

The author has tried to recreate the events, locales and conversations based on interactions with women leaders. Some conversations have been recreated and/or supplemented. To maintain anonymity in some instances, the names of individuals and places, the author may have changed some identifying characteristics and details such as physical properties, occupations, and places of residence. The author in no capacity represents any company, corporation, or brand mentioned in the book.

The author of this book disclaims liability for any loss or damage suffered by any person as a result of the information or content in this book. The information in this book is only for the purpose of motivating and inspiring women professionals and young girls to dream big. Any advice or recommendations are made without guarantee on the part of the author.

CHAPTER 1

A True Fighter Who Never Gives Up

This is the story of a girl who was inspired by her grandfather to aim for Chartered Accountancy as a career. She met her husband at work and now has a beautiful family with two teenage children. She lives her life on her terms and is never afraid to choose to work part-time whenever family or children need her, yet she made it to CFO positions in large multinational companies. She is a true fighter, taking on challenges head-on—both professionally and personally.

Let me introduce you to Kristina Isherwood, who is lovingly called Kris. She is a tall, beautiful, and intelligent woman and is brave enough to never give up in any circumstances. Kris and her identical twin sister, Katharine, were born in Carshalton, Surrey, in the United Kingdom, some 15 miles from London. Kris's father, Frederick, was born in South London and did his schooling during World War II. Most of the time, the children in his school studied while ducked under the desk as the air raids would happen at any time. He left school at the age of 15 and started from the ground up; he learnt his trade and eventually started an office furniture business. He expanded his business over the years with immense hard work and perseverance. Kris's mother, Yvonne, belongs to a wealthy Swedish family. Her family settled in London after World War II, and her father ran an imported furniture business. The furniture business was the connection

Photo of Kristina rowing

that led Fred and Yvonne to meet and subsequently get married. After marriage, Kris's father also bought a hotel on the south coast of England, which Kris's mother managed. Kris's parents were very hardworking and were at work most days while Kris and her twin sister stayed home with their Swedish grandmother.

Kris and Katharine always had a great time together as siblings and still do. As children, they were always available for each other, whether to discuss studies, homework or friends. Even today, Kris knows that her sister has got her back whenever required. They loved playing creative games with their friends. They would create a make-believe town with their friends, where all participants had roles to play. Katharine would pretend to run the school and the library. She eventually also chose a similar career and now works as a Head Teacher at a local primary school. Kris, on the other hand, would set up a market selling sweets, toys, and gifts. She would buy real candies from a shop with her pocket money, divide them, and pack them in fancy colourful packing. Kris would then sell them to her friends for thrice the original price and make money!

As Kris grew up, she realized how blessed she was to have a secure childhood with a good lifestyle, thanks to her parents, who worked hard to make that available for Katharine and her sister. Kris inherited this quality of being a sincere worker from her parents. Kris's grandfather, Gabriel, had come from Sweden as a migrant, trained as a Chartered Accountant and established an imported furniture business using his European connections. Whenever Kris met him, he shared stories of business and politics with her. Kris always found those conversations interesting, and she distinctly remembers her grandfather words even today – "Kris, my child, unless you try, you will never know whether you can achieve your goal or not; what have you got to lose?"

Kris studied economics at university, and her grandfather encouraged her to find an internship at one of the "Big Four" firms in London. She joined as an audit trainee in KPMG and not only cleared her exams in her first attempt but also rose fast in KPMG to subsequently become a Director, and was on a fast track to becoming a partner soon in a few years. During this time, she was offered a two-year secondment assignment to Sydney and then a two-year assignment in Zurich on her return to London. It was during her time in London, she met Andrew, who also worked for KPMG. They were married within 18 months after first meeting each other. Their honeymoon was spent in Sydney at the millennium celebrations, catching up with all her friends and colleagues from her time in Australia.

She had completed almost 13 years at KPMG when one of her clients, the CEO of Winterthur, a European insurance company, approached her with an offer to join them as CFO. Kris was very hesitant, and she thought about the offer for almost a week before saying yes. It wasn't an easy decision for Kris, as she had never stepped out of the KPMG world and was probably less than a year away from becoming a Partner, which had been her ambition.

Kris was only 31 years old when she joined Winterthur as the CFO. On her first day, she had set up the Monday team leadership meeting for finance and felt terrified. As she entered the meeting room, she faced at least 10 male colleagues, all much older than her and far more experienced.

Photo of Kristina

Hit with severe imposter syndrome and full of self-doubt, it was a case of really digging deep and repeatedly telling herself that '*I can do it, and I am good enough.*'

The next step was to meet her team that in total had 125 members. Once again, she had to step up and act as the leader. The most challenging part in the new work environment was that she had no peers to take advice or counselling from, unlike at KPMG, where she could consult many peers. She recognized that in this new environment she had to take the lead, working through the problems as a team, but essentially, she was the one who had to take the call. Occasionally she felt that it was a lonely place, but in the end, everything turned out well for Kris.

In four years at Winterthur, she partnered with the CEO and the other business leaders to refocus the business and move into a sustainable profit position. She also managed the company through a merger with AXA. Even though she enjoyed her work, the hardest part was to manage her firstborn son while having long working hours, and on some days, there seemed no respite. She had to work for at least 12 hours a day and travel on weekends. This was not sustainable for her with her little one-year-old son Ben, at home. She soon taught herself to empower others more and not micromanage all the outputs. She realized not everything needed to be her version of "perfect".

After this deal, Kris decided to take a year's break from her work, during which she had her second child, a beautiful baby girl. Kris' priority shifted; she was now looking out for profiles with the flexibility to work three days a week. She joined Fidelity International in a non-finance profile as a Chief Admin officer for Fidelity's UK Insurance business. Here she partnered with the Defined Contribution Pension (DC) business team to support the development of Fidelity's DC proposition and strategy. Within four months, she was able to provide inputs and refocus the strategic direction of the business, which was immensely satisfying. Despite this success, Kris aspired and loved more significant strategic roles and was also conscious that she had no desire to work five days a week with young children at home. Kris was offered the position of CFO of the UK & Europe region at Fidelity International within six months with the flexibility to operate on a four-days-a-week basis. The senior leadership was very impressed with Kris, and within a year, she was promoted as the Group CFO, running a global team of over 500 people again on a four-day-a-week basis.

Family and her children have always been important to Kris. Kris' son, Ben, was once part of a Christmas skit organized by his playschool, and Ben excitedly got ready in his Christmas costume for the play. As Kris was leaving for the office that day, he said, "Hey Mum, see you at school. I will wave at you when I am on stage; please do wave back!" Andrew was out of town for an assignment that day. Kris reached the office, and the CEO called an urgent meeting. During the meeting, Kris looked at her watch and hoped that she wouldn't get late for the play. Unfortunately, Kris was late, and by the time she reached school, the play had ended. She looked around; all the kids were hugging their parents while Ben was standing alone on stage and sobbing… This sight was difficult to bear, and she hugged him tightly. Kris apologized, "I am very sorry, and this will never happen again." As they were leaving, the teacher handed over the photo of Ben in the costume. Kris stuck that photo on her daily writing pad to remind herself each day that if she commits anything to her child, she will make sure that she fulfils it. She has never let her children down since.

As Kris became Fidelity's Group CFO, she ended up being on the plane, primarily long-distance flights, almost two weeks of the month. Andrew's job was also very demanding. Kris had to outsource so much of the typical household activities to others that there was a nanny, an ex-teacher to supervise homework, a cleaner, and a gardener. While her sister, who lived close to their home, also helped a lot, no one was really happy. Everything felt pressured; after a full-on day at work, everything else at home required even more organization.

One Wednesday night, when Kris reached home from the airport after a full-on three-day trip, the kids hugged her tightly and cried, "Mum, we miss you and Dad." Kris burst into tears after putting them to sleep. She sat with Andy and declared, "I think it can't work this way, our children are suffering because of us, and we are all miserable. On Monday, either I will resign, or you do so!!" Andy said, "Don't worry – Fidelity offers you more flexibility than what my company can ever offer. So, you should continue and let me speak to my leaders." On Monday morning, Andy discussed with his leaders that he wanted to take 12 months sabbatical leave. He was relieved within two weeks. A year after this discussion, he decided to resign, and now it has been more than eight years that he enjoys spending time with his children and supports Kris in her career wholeheartedly. The whole household is now a very happy place joined by their yellow Labrador, Cookie.

At the workplace, integrity is something that Kris values the most. Whenever she notices someone diverting from the company's agenda and focusing on an approach that does not have the potential to deliver maximum benefit to the organization, she doesn't shy away from having a candid conversation to give that message. As the CFO of the company, whether at Winterthur or Fidelity, Kris has elevated the finance team's role as a strategic partner and analytics centre to enable the future direction of the company. In the early days as Group CFO, Kris noticed that there were multiple teams across the global organization creating different versions of similar data. She then got a buy-in from the business that finance would be the holder of the golden source of all key data sets. This ensured integrity of strategic decision making. Finance teams then integrated themselves within business areas to deliver key information required by leaders. As a result, the meetings, instead of being focused on the integrity of the underlying data, became focused on the issue at hand.

In the year 2016, one day after successfully closing a business deal in Canada, Kris went back home to England. She was feeling exhausted, and even after a weekend's rest, she didn't feel energetic. At first, she dismissed this to the hectic weeks she had spent at work in what was one of her most stressful assignments. However, due to abundant caution, she decided to visit the doctor. The doctor advised some scans and tests. To Kris' surprise, the reports and scans diagnosed early stage of an aggressive form of breast cancer. Kris was shattered; it felt as if someone had pulled the ground beneath her feet. Andrew, her children, and her sister couldn't just stop their tears hearing this news. Kris decided to stay calm and researched the hospital and doctors who were most advanced in dealing with her type of cancer. She chose The Royal Marsden Hospital in London, receiving a course of treatment that was just three months post medical trials. It consisted of a targeted chemotherapy approach, a new biological drug called Herceptin, and radiotherapy sessions coupled with a few surgeries. Upon receipt of this knowledge, Kris focused on her to-do list at the office and spoke to her leader to break this news. Fidelity was incredibly supportive and offered all the assistance they could. She then met her finance leadership team and announced that she was going on a six-month break. Her heart was pounding hard as she left the office with good wishes from all her colleagues.

Kris was very clear in her mind that she would not give up and would fight cancer with a positive attitude. Kris and her sister have been doing a 10k run every Sunday for many years, and even after the news of cancer diagnosis, she decided to continue the run. It usually took her 50 mins to complete a 10k run, but as chemotherapy sessions started by the end of

12 weeks, she could only complete the run in 1 hour 20 mins. Kris didn't give up her passion for running. Every Monday, when she went to the hospital for her therapy, the oncologist would ask, "Kris!! How many minutes did it take this time?" Kris would excitingly share her run stats like a small kid.

As Kris would enter the therapy room with several bays with many patients and equipment around her, she would promise herself that she will come out of it for her family. Kris felt blessed to work for Fidelity as the company supported her during these tough times. In one of her chemotherapy sessions, the Senior Leader at Fidelity International arrived from Overseas to sit beside Kris. Kris was full of gratitude and a sense of belonging with the support from such a wonderful organization.

Those six months going in and out of operation theatre and therapy rooms made Kris realize that there is nothing more important than family and health in life. After six months, she went back to work at Fidelity and was grateful for all the support she received from her colleagues while she was away, but eager to start work again and focus on something else which was not cancer-related!

After nine years at Fidelity International as the CFO, Kris wanted to do something different, providing a new challenge. And that's when the Senior Management offered her the role as the CFO of Eight Roads, the venture capital arm of the Fidelity group. Kris was tasked with key responsibility to demerge and help restructure the business post the exit of senior management in 2019. Kris, with her expertise, led the demerger of Eight Roads from Fidelity International smoothly. She streamlined the governance processes and provided financial leadership through COVID-19, focusing on liquidity and realizing gains from certain investments. She is now thinking about her next challenge and has started rowing competitively. She says this is the hardest challenge yet!

Kris is a true fighter and never gives up in life.

Kris' leadership mantras are:

- Be yourself; every leadership style is unique. Be genuine. There is no magic formula. As a leader, you set an ethical standard and become an example to the whole organization.

- Treat people with respect; treat individuals as you would like to be treated.

- You can't succeed unless you try. What have you got to lose?

Chapter 2

You Have a Choice to Make

Just like it is said, *"Your life is a result of choices you make,"* here is a lady who made some hard choices in her life. As a young woman who had a degree in Chemical Engineering, but chose to build a career in finance, as a young mother who decided to miss a career advancement opportunity since she didn't want to move out from her city, also, as a senior professional who chose to resign as the CFO when the company's values didn't align with her values. At the age of 50, she chose to work for companies whose core business is to pay forward to the community. This is a story of a woman who made choices in life keeping her and her dear ones' priorities in mind. She was one of the first women in Brazil to be appointed as the CFO of a listed company. Since then, she has held various COO and CFO positions in companies in Latin America.

Let me introduce you to Cynthia Hobbs, a lady full of infectious energy despite being in her 50s. She has excellent networking skills, and when you read her story, you will learn that she got jobs in her career with the help of her strong network. Integrity is the most important value to her. She believes integrity is the core value of a successful and happy life. Having integrity means being totally honest and truthful in every part of your life. She advocates that "The quality of the person you are is determined by how well you live up to the values that are most important to you." Her story will inspire you in many ways.

Photo of Cynthia (middle) with her parents

Cynthia was born in Belo Horizonte in Brazil. She loved Mathematics as a subject and liked numbers during her school days. She had developed a rational way of thinking early on, which helped her crack complex mathematical problems with ease. She was keen to apply for a Mathematics honours course in a university until her mother, Sylce, asked her a question one day, "What profession will you choose with a Math degree?"

Cynthia dwelt on this important question. In those days, with a Math degree, one could only become a teacher in Brazil. That profession unfortunately wasn't paid good money and Cynthia wanted to earn good money for a stable lifestyle. Hence, she decided to take up engineering and got a degree as a Chemical Engineer. The most interesting part is that she never happened to work as an engineer in her entire life!

After completing engineering, she felt the need for further studies to get a good job. She went to Switzerland and completed her MBA from City University in Zurich. After her studies, she returned to São Paulo and got a job at Ambev, the largest Brazilian brewing company. She enjoyed working in finance and worked on an NYSE listing project. In Ambev, everyone worked hard, and each employee had skin in the game for the success of the company. Everyone at the workplace proudly wore their Ambev logo T-shirts. They had literally taken an oath that they would never drink any beverage of another brand as a sign of loyalty to the company!

During a visit to a friend's house one evening, Cynthia was offered Coke. While Cynthia took the Coke can in her hands, her inner soul cried, "How can you drink Coke? It's a beverage of non-Ambev brand!" Cynthia put down the can on the table and politely refused the drink, giving some random reason. She worked diligently and often for long hours. This dedication helped her create a solid foundation in the early years of her career.

Cynthia got married to Cesar Pinho, and after eight years, they were blessed with a baby boy, Matheus. The culture at Ambev was warm and friendly, and every week Cynthia had happy hours evening outings with her colleagues. Everyone at the workplace had great bonding. Today, even though it has been 20 years that Cynthia left Ambev, she is still connected with her ex-colleagues. They all meet for drinks every couple of months, even today! Matheus was only a year old when Cynthia was selected for a prestigious course along with a few other colleagues. The course required her to travel for a week, four times in the year. Cynthia didn't want to leave her toddler baby at home, so whenever she travelled, she took Matheus along with his nanny. During the daytime, when she was busy in the training, Matheus would stay back in the hotel along with his nanny. In the evening, during dinner time, Cynthia and her colleagues would sing songs and fly paper aeroplanes to make Matheus eat his food as he was a very fussy eater. By the end of the year, on their fourth trip, Matheus was familiar with all of his mom's colleagues that were a part of the training.

When Matheus turned two, Cynthia was offered a promotion, but the role was outside São Paulo. Cynthia told her leader that she needed some time to revert as Cesar had a good job in São Paulo. Cynthia came back home, and Matheus hugged her. She had dinner with Matheus and Cesar and thought, '*What choice should I make? Should I accept the offer and be with my family only on weekends?*' She thought about it the whole night and then decided to reject the offer as her family mattered to her the most. While she had already made her choice, she was a little upset about letting go of a good opportunity. Cynthia also felt that she was limiting her learning and exposure in the same company in São Paulo. She decided to explore opportunities outside Ambev after working there for almost six years.

After her graduation, Cynthia had been an active participant in the social circle of finance professionals in São Paulo. She had networked well with industry leaders, and some of them were her trusted advisers. This helped her land a job as the Head of Investor relations in Ultra, a Brazilian company in the fuel distribution sector that was listed in Brazil and New York. She managed the Investor Relations and Planning of the company. Cynthia handled multiple finance profiles in Ultra and was soon promoted to the role of Finance and Administrative Director. She added multiple portfolios in her work experiences such as implementing ERP systems, handling tax planning and filings, internal controls, and SOX compliance roles.

The work culture at Ultra was very different from Ambev. It was a very professional environment where she never had a single happy hours get-together with her colleagues. Formal official lunches were preferred over evening drinks or dinner parties. Though Cynthia missed Ambev days, what made her stay in Ultra for almost 10 years was that she had great portfolios providing her with the opportunity to work with senior leaders. Cynthia developed a keen eye for detail and data analytics skills which helped her get senior finance roles.

After a decade in Ultra, Cynthia was at a point in her life when she was questioning herself – what could she do next? Her son had grown up, and she felt she was ready to take on newer challenges in life. She chose to work in a startup environment which would help her get an end-to-end knowledge of business operations.

Cynthia joined a startup in Brazil as their COO. This was not a core finance job, and it wasn't an easy move. For a person who had worked for the first 16 years in her career in big companies, it wasn't easy to adapt to the working environment of a startup. It was only a month in the company when Cynthia had to get their corporate bank account opened along with credit lines. Cynthia called up her bank relationship managers from previous companies. She was surprised that relationships with bankers, which she thought were personal, were just based on position that she held in the previous organization. She realized that when you work for a company with billions of dollars of sales, you have access to every Bank in Brazil, but when you work for a startup, you will have to make multiple visits to bank branches to get your credit lines approved. For almost a year, every morning,

Cynthia used to question herself, *'Have I made the right career decision?'* But whenever she had emotions of regret, she would remind herself, *'Were you happy living that monotonous life with no bigger purpose of paying it forward to communities?'* Today, when Cynthia looks back at this decision, she feels that this was the right choice she made which helped her succeed and adapt in different environments. She led the operations and finance of the company, working closely with the founding members on business strategies. After a few years, she also worked on negotiations and sales of the company. She gained the experience of working in a much smaller company having to grow the business with limited resources. This experience made Cynthia a well-rounded professional ready to take up senior leadership roles.

Later that year, she was appointed as a CFO by a large company in Healthcare. She was one of the first women in Brazil to be appointed as the CFO of a listed company. Almost every Brazilian newspaper covered the news of her

Photo of Cynthia with her family

appointment. She didn't take this role for granted and worked hard each day to prove herself and groomed a strong finance team under her. She believed in transparent communication at all levels in the organization and ensured that the finance team is seen as a partner by all stakeholders. She worked on multiple challenging projects. One of them involved review, redesign, and automation of the processes in reducing the closing cycle. She could partner and influence multiple teams in the company leading to a reduction in the accounts closing period from 25 to 7 working days. Another big learning project for her was the issuance of two large multi-million-dollar debentures during her tenure.

While on the professional front, she was enjoying and delivering a lot, she constantly had a nagging urge to work for a bigger purpose in life and paying it back to communities. After two years, one day, she chose that her values matter to her the most. She felt that working in an environment where her values were not aligned with the company, wasn't right. She decided to leave the company and resigned. It wasn't an easy decision because it's never easy to find jobs at senior levels.

Soon she joined Schneider Electric Brazil as VP Operations, and this was the second time in her career when she didn't have a finance profile. According to Cynthia, Schneider was a great company with a lot of emphasis on values like respect and integrity. Cynthia felt that Schneider had a wonderfully inclusive environment where women leaders had a voice on the table and no gender bias. Usually, in Brazil, women professionals are not treated at par with their male colleagues. Many times, in her working career, Cynthia felt that her views and thoughts were not heard attentively by senior leaders as compared to those of her male colleagues. Often in meetings, being the only female in the room, she was interrupted in her speech by her male colleagues without any apology. At Schneider, on the other hand, females had equal opportunity to speak and share their views, and decisions were not gender-biased. The period from 2015 to 2017 was one of the worst financial crises that Brazil's economy had seen, with an unemployment rate of 12%! At Schneider, she was given the key responsibility of restructuring, and she had to make hard decisions of layoffs. It was a very challenging phase, but she ensured that the impacted employees were treated respectfully and maintained transparency through frequent communication. She helped them negotiate the best severance packages. When Cynthia was given this team, the employee engagement score was 56%, and after three years, the score had climbed up to 74%. She could improve the scores despite 33% headcount being laid off.

At the age of 50, she moved to a non-profit organization called Renova Foundation as their CFO. It was now the time for her to live her dream of working towards the community around her. The Renova Foundation was founded in the year 2016 to mobilise the repatriation of funds for the damages caused by the collapse of the Mariana dam.

In November 2015, the Mariana dam disaster news flashed in news channels across the globe. This disaster created a humanitarian crisis as hundreds were displaced and several cities in Brazil along the Doce River suffered water shortages. The Renova Foundation's programmes were skilfully designed to provide help on two main fronts: remediation and compensation. The first goal was to restore and re-establish communities and resources affected by the dam collapse, while the second goal aimed to compensate for what could not be remediated.

Cynthia relocated from São Paulo to the State of Minas Gerais, where Mariana is located in Brazil. Cynthia, as a CFO, was responsible for controlling the disbursements. She was also responsible for one of the most challenging programmes involving paying indemnity to families impacted by the disaster. These negotiations were never easy. The affected families were full of anger and hate as they had lost their homes and belongings and were displaced.

Cynthia recalls one such compensation hearing at the office premises. "A young couple entered the room, the female was pregnant, and they sat across the table. The couple shared their story on how their ancestral home had collapsed during the tragedy and how they were forced to live their last four years in a rental home. Given their earnings, they could never afford to buy their own home. The mediator shared the good news with them that they had been allotted land and would be given money to build their home." As Cynthia handed over the land documents and cheque, the pregnant young lady and the young man had tears rolling down their cheeks and thanked Cynthia. Over this period, Cynthia met several families impacted by the disaster, listened to them, and worked on genuine disbursements. This was the most satisfying part of her job, and she felt she was giving back to communities in some way.

After three years, she went through a very difficult moment in her personal life when her mother, Sylce, died. Sylce had always been a great pillar of support for her. While Cynthia was away from home at work, Sylce had always provided support to her family and taken care of Matheus. Cynthia decided that she needed to be closer to her family. Cynthia decided to move back to São Paulo and started exploring job opportunities. She continued to focus on finding an organization that aligned with her values.

After some months of her return, she joined as the CFO at GetNinjas, an Internet startup company that is a local services marketplace in LATAM, with over 500 different services categories, such as cleaners, private lessons, painters, plumbers, and hundreds of other services. She feels proud that in current times when over 13 million people in Brazil are unemployed, her company helps people find jobs and earn a living for themselves. Working in a technology company was a dream for her, especially in a business that helps people find new jobs. Recently GetNinjas announced their Initial Public Offering (IPO) and got listed on the Brazil Stock exchange.

Cynthia is proud of what she has achieved in her life and is a happy soul on earth.

Cynthia's leadership mantras are:

- Leadership starts with trust. Communication and transparency are keys to building trust.

- Respect people around you.

- Believe in meritocracy – reward and acknowledge high performing talent, differentiate sharply.

- Integrity should be part of your character and not additional.

- Work with passion and love what you do.

- Have the humility to listen to different opinions and willingness to change your opinion.

CHAPTER 3

The Courage to Speak Up

A teenage girl gathered the courage to tell her father that her dream was to become an accountant instead of a doctor. A married woman drew courage to tell her family that she can't be only a homemaker and wants to pursue her career. A senior professional spoke courageously to tell her boss that she was struggling to juggle as CFO of three companies because of a lack of trust between the CEOs. This is the story of a woman who was hired as CFO at the young age of 26 with very little experience in finance roles. Like an Army General sent to war without real-life battle experience, she courageously fought each challenge that came her way, and today, she is a respected name in the CFO community in India. She didn't take her CFO title for granted and even today believes in proving herself each day with courage and conviction.

Let me introduce you to Kriti Makhija. Kriti is a finance professional who has worked towards finding the larger purpose of her life. When you would read her LinkedIn blogs on "living more intentionally," "leadership tips," and "thinking positively," you will find words that instantly touch your heart and brain. She is a doting mother, wife, daughter-in-law, and daughter. A person who has always paved her path and never been bogged by stereotypes, biases, or patriarchal mindsets. The biggest testament to this is that ever since her father died, her mother lives with her family along with her in-laws. You can imagine her courage and a heart full of love that takes everyone along with her.

Photo of Kriti (extreme right) with her family

Kriti was born in Ludhiana. Her father was in the Indian Army, and her mother was a teacher. She was the younger child with an older brother. Her parents raised both kids with equality. In her upbringing, she was always told to *'dream big'*. She was never told that she couldn't do certain things because she was a girl. Her father was her idol since childhood, and he wanted Kriti to become a doctor. Kriti started living her father's dream. She was very good at academics, but when she reached high school, despite her excellent grades, she realized that science did not inspire her. She hated the sight of blood, and she feared even dissecting a cockroach in the biology lab. She realized that she didn't want to be a doctor and hence couldn't fulfil her father's dream. Instead, she was fascinated with numbers and was happy when she was doing complex mathematics problems like statistics and algebra. With this clarity, one evening, when her father came back from work, Kriti gathered the courage to talk to him about what she really wanted for her career. She was sad as she knew that her father would be heartbroken. At that moment, as a young girl, she spoke to her father about 'what she wants'. Her father indeed was heartbroken, but she knew that she wanted to be an accounting professional and communicated it with courage, clarity, and empathy. Her father supported her and backed her wholeheartedly to fulfil her dream. He realized that she needed exposure to a big city. He moved to Delhi so that she could pursue her graduation in commerce from Delhi University and later took early retirement so that there was no disruption in her education. Kriti's dream was now her father's dream!!

Kriti enrolled for the Chartered Accountancy (CA) course at the Indian Institute of Chartered Accountants. As part of the course, the students are required to intern in an accounting firm. She was successfully selected for an internship at Price Waterhouse (PW) Delhi office (now PricewaterhouseCoopers or PwC). She was thrilled as it wasn't easy to get selected in a Big 4 firm. The success was sweeter for her as this was on the basis of her own merits, without using any references or connections. She reached home excited and shared the exhilarating news with her mom; seeing her ecstatic, her mom was happy and congratulated her, but was quite perplexed as she had no idea what PW was and confused it with PWD

(Public Works Department). Her mom went back to her father and checked with him, "I believed she was planning to do CA, so what will she do at PWD?"

Kriti was thriving in her CA course with an enriching practical experience at PW (now PwC). Soon after her intermediate exams, she went on an extended outstation audit in the hinterlands of India and met her life partner, Sumit, for the first time at the Delhi railway station in a kind of reel life situation. The person turned out to be her manager on the assignment, and after months of working together, they fell in love! Being her authentic self, within days of committing to Sumit, Kriti told her parents about her desire to marry him and soon after clearing her CA final exams, they got married.

Then started the next chapter in Kriti's life. While her husband's family was loving, they had a traditional mindset, with no daughter-in-law from a professional background in the family. It was a big joint family set-up, and they lived in Delhi. The women in the family were either homemakers or in teaching or government jobs, or non-professional jobs, which are classically seen as easy or less intensive. Sumit idolized his mom, a home maker, and wished Kriti to be a home maker, too. Kriti, after finishing her internship, did not take up a job. Meanwhile, soon after their marriage, her husband got an overseas assignment, and she happily accompanied him.

Once back in India, Kriti realized that being a full-time homemaker was not for her. She wasn't happy spending the whole day at home managing just the household work, which, if managed well, did not take more than a couple of hours with some help. She was raised to be gainfully occupied with a deep sense to contribute to home, society, and most importantly, grow as a person. Kriti remembered the juncture that she had reached in her teenage days when she had a heart to heart with her father to tell him that she can't live his dreams as they were not aligned with her dreams.

One weekend, she told her husband about her aspirations to work and how unhappy she would be if she were just to be a homemaker. With her life partner aligned, the next logical step was to talk to her parents-in-law and make them part of her dream. Living in a large joint family, she encouraged them to be part of her dream because it mattered to her. While she gave her commitment to them to balance work along with home priorities, she also asked for their support to do so in her journey ahead. Perhaps they saw that desire and spark 'to be' in Kriti, and they all aligned with her thinking. And once that was done, they backed her and supported her to the extent of also talking about it proudly with other family members. Soon even the ones who did not support that decision started supporting her wholeheartedly. And the added advantage thereafter was the family's changed mindset; now everyone wanted a professionally qualified daughter-in-law, like Kriti.

A trailblazer of change in her space, she has thrived on authenticity, honesty, compassion, and thinking out of the box and her family loves her for being her. As a staunch believer in the power within, a change maker, she does not care about 'looking good' and complying mindlessly, but believes in 'doing good', and that is what makes her unique and effective in all her roles. And this unique quality is reflective in her personality, even in normal conversation, and what inspires many, and leaves footprints in the memories and hearts of those who meet her.

Kriti didn't have very high career ambitions at that time and joined back PwC in the Tax team. She was soon blessed with a baby boy but continued working with PwC after her maternity break. While everyone at PwC knew her strengths and performance capabilities, most of her bosses were her husband's friends. The folks who were her bosses during the daytime in the office would be friends having drinks together in the evening. This was uncomfortable for Kriti, and she felt as if she was having an identity crisis.

Photo of Kriti

She scouted for jobs and joined Max Ateev in a classic accounting job. She was enjoying her work and living her dream, but little did she know what was in store for her in the future. Almost a year later, on her 25th birthday, she got the surprising news that her company was closing all operations. She was despondent; she cried utterly unsure of her future on her birthday. When a company is winding up, the finance team is the last team to leave. Kriti too was amongst the 3-member finance team working directly with the CFO on winding-up procedures of the company. Subsequently, when the CFO also left within a few months, she worked directly with the CEO for the last few months of the organization. She worked diligently, assuming way higher responsibilities than what was expected of her, given her limited experience. The CEO saw that spark of excellence, and one day he left a post-it note on her desk instructing her to meet Prema, Principal & Founder and Ashwani, CEO of Genesis PR. As a junior, and very unlike her usual self, she couldn't gather the courage to ask her boss, the purpose of the meeting and assumed that it probably was for a vendor settlement!

On the day of the meeting, Prema was unavailable, but Kriti met other leaders at Genesis. Through several meetings, she was asked lots of questions by the people she met, while she had no clue of their intent. Unable to hold it any further, she then inquired the 'purpose' of these questions and was told that she was being interviewed and had been selected for the role of CFO at Genesis. Kriti was just 26 years old then with barely 2.5 years of work experience; she was dumbfounded with exhilaration and fear as she had no clue what it took to be a 'CFO'. One of the leaders at Genesis who interviewed Kriti that day was Ashwani, with whom she worked extensively for a decade.

Kriti joined Genesis in November 2002 and continues to work there to date. Genesis is now one of the most reputed communications firms in the country. Genesis became a part of a global network and a listed organization in 2006 and then diversified further to be an integrated communication company with several brands folding under the Genesis umbrella.

Genesis is led by an inspiring woman Chairperson & Founder—Prema Sagar, who has inspired Kriti each day to be more and have a higher purpose in life. On day one in the company, she taught her the importance of building a relationship and always treating all stakeholders—clients, employees, and vendors with respect as partners for business success.

Taking up the role of a CFO was a pivotal moment in Kriti's life. She worked hard each day to learn 'how to be a leader' while sharpening her saw by building her domain knowledge, building a team and in the process learning from her mistakes all along. On the personal front, her son was now four years old. Her family was of great support and were aligned to her dream and career. They not only supported her but also empowered her to take up such a challenging job and grow in her career. She hired house help and trained them to take care of all household chores and used to plan her whole week in advance.

On the work front, Kriti handled new challenges to step up the learning curve at a fast pace. Alongside Prema and Ashwani, she led the mergers & acquisition negotiations with a global firm called WPP for acquiring her firm. It was not highs all the time. Life does not work that way. It is indeed a roller coaster and had its equal shares of low, both personal and professional. Kriti did fail multiple times, but she bounced back stronger each time and rose higher with the resilience in her character.

Meanwhile, due to a restructuring at WPP, an additional company was formed in India, led by another CEO. Kriti was appointed as the CFO of this new company along with her existing company. This was truly an exciting opportunity. But Kriti now had two bosses to report to, and there were many moments of conflicting meetings, deadlines, and sometimes even business conflicts that were hard to manage. All of this took a huge emotional and mental toll on Kriti's psychological health. Being a person who never quits, Kriti tried her best to handle the turmoil at hand while delivering great results in both organizations, but, after five years of chaos in this role that accompanied emotional scrutiny and psychological stress, Kriti realized that she needs to stand up and have the courage to speak to her bosses. It is not easy for any senior professional to have such conversations with their mentors. She had a candid conversation with both the CEOs, explaining the challenges and why she can't continue in conflicting roles. Kriti went back to group leadership and said "It's not possible for me to continue as CFO of two companies and report to two bosses." She was asked to choose which company would she want to continue as CFO. Coming from a culture of loyalty and values and with a deep sense of belonging, her choice was very clear, and she chose to be with Genesis BCW.

Like her previous experiences of having the courage to speak to her father and then her family about what made her happy, she found that communicating with authenticity always helps. When she reflects on this phase, she feels that she should have gathered courage much earlier to speak to her bosses.

Her story of courage to keep pushing boundaries doesn't end here. One Saturday afternoon during a family brunch, she received a phone call from Prema and was told that starting Monday, she was to be the mentor for the three new Centres of Expertise (COEs) of Genesis BCW. Kriti was taken aback, and her mind started running in various directions of why, what, how she was befitting to that role with no experience in sales or marketing or business incubation. Come Monday, Kriti spoke to Prema about her apprehensions. Prema told her that she believed that her capabilities as a leader are far more nuanced than just being a CFO, a domain expert. And with Prema's words of belief and her own courage to act started a new chapter of Kriti's evolution as a mentor. She started with mentoring three COEs, the growth engines of the company, to incubate and bring them to a scale and then over the years incubated a few more. This additional responsibility taught her to appreciate the business side of the organization. It also shifted her focus to overall business strategy and management from the classic CFO role of managing and monitoring the financial health as well as governance of the company.

In the last six years, Kriti has incubated four business units in Genesis, actively contributing to the growth engine of the company. She evolved herself constantly and ensured that she learnt new skills consistently. The business cycle understanding has also helped her to become a better CFO with a better ability to partner in business strategies. She was also able to empower her finance team and helped them grow. She enjoyed seeing her team members climb the ladder of success and celebrated team members' small wins, which kept them motivated. This made her realize the happiness of standing in a corner and clapping loudest with a smile on her face at the success of team members.

Kriti has, over the years, also realized the importance of emotional support at the workplace. The year 2006 was one of the most challenging phases in Kriti's family life. Her husband and his family were caught in a fierce legal battle. Her bosses at work and colleagues provided her emotional support during this tough phase. This helped her build a stronger bond at the workplace. Whenever any of Kriti's team members are going through a tough phase, she makes sure to provide that same emotional support to them.

A few years back, Kriti lost her father, and that was one of the most catastrophic moments in her life. She was devastated as she had lost her life's idol. A void that was very hard to fill. At home, she appeared to be strong to provide strength to her mother to deal with the loss. But could not maintain the brave stance at work and would often break down. Her teams engulfed her in their love, and their support helped her get back on her feet. She vividly remembers a young colleague walking up to her with a comforting smile to say that Genesis BCW is her work family and is there to support her in this darkest hour of life.

Over the last 18+ years, Kriti has learnt the importance of building and nurturing relationships. She believes in creating an environment where everyone thrives. She is a great fan of **"Ubuntu"**, an African philosophy that emphasizes 'being self through others'. It is a form of humanism that can be expressed in the phrase 'I am because of who we all are'.

Kriti currently is focusing on finding her *ikigai*, a reason for being, for the next chapter of her life.

Kriti's leadership mantras:

- Embrace the 'I'. Be your authentic self and be proud of who you are. Know your core set of values and beliefs that you always stand by consistently.

- Change your thoughts, change your world. The only limits you have are the ones that you place on yourself.

- Be a woman leader and establish your presence. Femininity and Leadership are not contradictory but complementary.

- Get out of your comfort zone, take risks, and grow. Have the courage to speak, to act and to be.

- Find your champions. Your confidence, impact, and positivity will help you in marching ahead, and "champions" can change your trajectory.

- Follow the framework of brutal prioritization. Don't try to be a superwoman! We can have it all but not in one day.

- Take responsibility for your life. Your higher purpose and being part of a larger story create an impact not just for you. Try creating opportunities and open doors for others; that's the POWER in You.

CHAPTER 4

Convert Each Challenge into an Opportunity

A young woman married to an Indian Air Force officer managed her work-life beautifully with young kids despite her husband being posted away from home often. When most wives of defence professionals prefer to accompany their husbands, she chose to tread a different path and continued to focus on her career and worked hard towards it. This is the story of a woman who converted each challenge in her career into an opportunity to become the only woman CFO in the male-dominated automobile industry in India.

Let me introduce you to Sneha Oberoi, a simple kind-hearted person with humble values. If you Google her name, you will find her blogs and views on multiple finance topics in premium financial newspapers in India. She is also a regular feature on ET-CFO.com. Sneha is the mother of two beautiful daughters, Maanya and Ahana, and lives with her husband, Manish Oberoi, in Gurgaon, Haryana, India.

Sneha is a fitness freak and starts her day with power yoga. She loves cycling and running. Being a CFO to her means mentoring, guiding, and providing support to key managerial personnel and stakeholders for driving business growth. Sneha has always made sure that she spends quality time with her daughters on weekends. There were many instances when she couldn't join them for their school function or Parent-teacher meet. She had to teach her kids that their mother is different from other ladies who were full-time homemakers. Over the years, her kids understood this fact and adjusted. Today both the daughters are super proud of their mother as they see her being covered regularly in newspapers.

Sneha's grandparents had settled in Delhi in India after migrating from Pakistan at the time of the India-Pakistan partition. Her parents, Baldev Raj Sharma and Sharda Sharma, also went through many struggles in life, but made sure that their kids received the best education and had big dreams for themselves. Sneha's father was in the Indian Air Force, and her mother was a strong lady who took care of her kids when her husband was posted outside of Delhi.

Sneha did her schooling in Delhi, and her mother inspired her to become a working professional and do well for herself. Sneha's elder sister Neeru used to help Sneha with her homework and studies. Neeru always guided Sneha on what professional options she could choose when she reached high school. Sneha took commerce stream in the 11th standard. Though she loved accounting, a career in finance never fascinated her since it only comprised of old traditional bookkeeping back then. She completed her graduation in commerce with honours from Delhi University. She successfully cleared the exam to become a Cost Accountant while completing her industrial training from Maruti Udyog Ltd. During this time, there came a big change in the Indian industry, the economy was opening and the finance leaders were becoming important in the organization. They started to play a critical role in decision making. This fascinated Sneha to explore her career in finance. After her qualification, she joined Price Waterhouse Coopers (PWC) India in Delhi.

Within a year, her parents got her married. It was an arranged marriage where her father found a suitable match for her. Her husband, Manish, was then working in the Indian Air Force just like her father. Manish's job demanded on-site posting to different cities in India. Sneha remembered those

Photo of Sneha (extreme left) with her daughters and husband

days when Sneha and her siblings would stay alone with their mother in Delhi, and their dad would be on a 'posting' serving the county. That feeling made her incredibly proud of both her parents for playing their roles so beautifully. Sneha too decided to stay in the Delhi NCR region with her in-laws and chose to pursue her career further. A year after marriage, she was blessed with her first daughter, Maanya. During this period, her parents and in-laws supported Sneha by taking care of Maanya when she was out for work.

After working for over five years in PWC and getting experience in various automation and automobile industries, she moved to Volvo Car India as a core member of the team responsible for setting up the finance processes of Volvo cars in India. This profile provided her with an opportunity to work on pricing, budgeting, and forecasting as a Business Controller.

In the year 2009, Ford sold off Volvo to a Chinese company, and this required her to contribute to the number crunching for the M&A deal. This was a critical process and involved irregular working hours due to the different time zones involved. Sneha, who was pregnant with her second child during this time, used to bring Maanya to the office sometimes during long workdays, as Manish was posted outside Delhi at that time. Her boss and colleagues were very supportive and provided her flexibility to get her daughter at work. Maanya used to spend time in the office doing her homework or playing some board games with the administrative staff of the office. Once Sneha was on a video conference call in a board room with colleagues across the globe, when Maanya just entered the room and asked in a loud voice, "Mummy, please order Pizza; I am very hungry." Everyone on the calls just smiled and excused Sneha to order something for Maanya. Sneha created a wonderful support system for Maanya not only at home with her mother and mother-in-law's support but also at work with the help of her colleagues. Her husband has always been supportive in managing and caring for the kids, and that gave Sneha time to focus on her profession.

After three months of maternity break, post Ahana's birth, Sneha joined Volvo Auto India Private Limited to work with a new leadership team and was soon promoted as the CFO of Volvo India. In her first stint as the CFO of a multinational automobile company, she took all the responsibilities of managing the finalization of the separation of Volvo India from Ford and set up a robust finance department. She was responsible for ERP implementation, taxation, transfer pricing, infrastructure technology (IT) department, and taking care of legal and compliance requirements of the newly formed company in India. She also had additional responsibilities as a Human Resources (HR) head, managing the strategies to attract and hire top talent in the market. Sneha was given all these responsibilities at a very young age. In the past, she had amply displayed her skills in being able to work and coordinate with different departments in the organization.

Sneha rose to this senior position rapidly, and many of her peers became her subordinates. She also got her dedicated cabin. Once, one of her ex-peers commented to her, "Sneha, you have gone far from us." Sneha reverted, "I am still near to your heart." After that instance, she made a conscious effort to have lunch or evening tea break with staff on the floor but at the same time maintaining a balance that everyone was aware of their roles and responsibilities.

When an expat joined as the new Managing Director (MD) of Volvo India, Sneha worked with him to make him aware of the Indian automobile sector's nuances. She partnered with him to create an India sales strategy until the Head of Sales was appointed. During her five years tenure as a CFO, the company saw substantial growth in India. Managing such a demanding, complex role wasn't easy with young kids, but luckily Manish got posted back in Delhi. She was able to give her best at work with her husband's support. After five years as CFO in India, Volvo offered Sneha an elevated overseas finance role which was unfortunately not feasible for her to take up considering her family priorities. She let that opportunity go keeping faith that more such career opportunities would come her way in the future, and they surely did. At the same time, Manish took voluntary retirement from the Indian Air Force, and she thought of exploring another CFO opportunity outside the Automobile Industry.

Sneha joined Wockhardt Hospitals Ltd. as their CFO, but this position was based out of Mumbai in India. Given that Maanya was in her 10th grade, which is a crucial academic year in the Indian education system, Manish decided to stay back in Delhi NCR with their two daughters, and Sneha relocated alone to Mumbai. Sneha stayed in Mumbai, shuttling between two cities while managing the role successfully. It was a tough time for Hospitals when the Indian Government announced demonetization on 8th November 2016. Sneha converted this challenge into an opportunity and helped the organization handle the cash flow crisis. She created strategies that helped the company stay afloat with sufficient working capital cash without any additional finance charges from banks. During the time of demonetization, the tax authorities in India were closely monitoring all transactions in India to ensure that illegal money was not channelled into the banking system using unethical practices. Sneha created detailed guidelines for hospital chain's cashiers to ensure that such unethical practices wouldn't happen. The branch in charge shared weekly reports with Sneha, through which she ensured adherence. Sneha is proud that during her tenure, they didn't get a single notice from the tax authorities, and no frauds were reported. Along with taking care of demonetization, within six months of joining the organization, she made the cash flow system so robust that the hospital did not have to ask for cash support from its parent organization Wockhardt Pharma. Even though she enjoyed her work in Mumbai, it was difficult for her kids to cope up without their mother. Ahana being very small at that time especially missed Sneha a lot. Sneha decided to return and began exploring opportunities in the Delhi NCR region.

In July 2018, Sneha returned to the automobile sector in the NCR region as the CFO and VP administration at Suzuki Motorcycle India Pvt Ltd. This was an elevated CFO profile along with responsibilities of IT, Legal, HR, Administration, Employee relations, Export logistics, Taxation and Compliance. The new thing to learn here was to handle employee relations in a unionized environment. Sneha had earlier worked only with white-collared employees, and this was her first experience of dealing with blue-collar employees. But with such a vast experience she knew the art of managing diverse personalities in different situations. Many times, Sneha has gauged that stress in the meeting room is aired through the voice tone and body language and quickly pivoted her

Photo of Sneha's mother – Sharda Sharma

leadership style to control the situation ensuring that the meeting ends on a polite note. As per her experience, there is one thing that a manager must understand, irrespective of whether the team member is white-collared or blue. One needs to have the skill of listening and providing a solution, and if one is unable to provide a solution at that point in time, then one should ask for time but make sure to solve the problem.

Throughout her journey as a CFO, Sneha has continued mentoring and guiding different teams in the organization. She has always believed that learning is a continuous process, and she herself never stopped learning. She undertook a one-year senior management programme from IIM Calcutta and various other senior management courses from Wharton and ISB to polish her managerial skills from time to time. Sneha believes that such management courses help one to brush up on the theoretical framework for leadership, which help you evolve to be a better leader. In these courses, Sneha got an opportunity to interact with peer leaders in the industry. She got to understand that everyone had similar challenges, and she wasn't alone. This helped her boost her morale when faced with problems.

Sneha has been proactive to anticipate the impact of changes under a Volatile, Uncertain, Complex and Ambiguous (VUCA) environment. She always converted challenges into opportunities by investing in and creating dynamic leaders within various cross-functional teams of the organization. Sneha believes in giving timely candid feedback and improvement areas to her colleagues rather than waiting for performance appraisal meetings. She does this successfully by creating a safe environment for her team where everyone can trust each other. She also shares information transparently and communicates clearly and candidly with her team members.

The year 2020 COVID-19 crisis required her to pivot on multiple dimensions. When the Indian Government announced a nationwide lockdown in the last week of March 2020, Sneha and her finance team were in the midst of annual financial closing while the headquarters of the company in Japan was open. The other priority for Sneha at that time was to ensure the safety of her employees in India. In response to the crisis, Sneha formed a senior management risk committee that met online daily to assess the situation, take actions for work from home, manage the P&L, and reset the goals along with ruthless prioritization. She made sure the MD and Board of Directors of the company were informed on a regular basis. During these times, she followed the mantra of staying calm, thinking, and then taking action. COVID-19 taught everyone new ways of working and adapting. As HR head, she had to ensure that employees remained motivated as there was fear amongst the staff of losing jobs. In one of the meetings, she asked all leaders on call to step up and guide, groom, and motivate employees with empathy. As the lockdown was lifted, she worked with business heads on return to office policies ensuring new safety standards, enabling manufacturing units to open. As the IT head, she had to ensure a sustainable working environment for employees in support functions, ensuring data accessibility along with data security.

As employees started returning to the workplace, all the line managers were given instructions on Do's and Don'ts to ensure that social distancing norms and mask hygiene culture are followed. The mantra was to constantly keep reminding everyone at the workplace to follow COVID precaution norms.

Sneha believes that for any working woman, the biological clock for motherhood, career, and family responsibilities are all at their peak in the 30s. A great support system at home and office can help women flourish and grow in their careers. Sneha's mother inspired her since childhood to dream big and aim for heights. At every milestone of success in her career, Sneha feels so grateful and blessed for what her mother has done for her. While there is a saying that "Behind every successful man, there is a woman," Sneha believes strongly that "Behind every successful woman, there is a husband and a tribe of family members."

Sneha Oberoi's leadership mantras are:

- Be a learner in life.
- As a leader, keep evolving and take new challenges.
- Listen to everyone, be nimble, check facts and react accordingly.
- Be a leader instead of a commanding manager.
- Stay humble; always have high integrity.

- Lead by example.

- Define a vision for the team and take everyone along.

- Always give timely feedback.

- Your team can make or break you; always respect your team.

CHAPTER 5

The Art of *Savoir-Faire* across Different Continents

A little girl born in Northern France who haven't even visted Paris until she reached high school had no idea that she would make an international career. She worked across different continents and in diverse finance roles to climb up the corporate ladder. Her husband also held CFO roles, and both managed their careers along with family commitments. Read this story to know how this girl with a dream to settle in the United States of America (USA) ended up being a CFO in companies in Japan. You may be wondering how a French-speaking person would have settled in Japanese culture and that too in the pre-google era? This real-life story is about Christine Meguro, who adapted to different cultures to be a successful CFO leading a happy life.

Christine Meguro was born in a traditional family in a city in Northern France. Her mother was a homemaker and her father a businessman. She was the eldest of the three daughters in the family. In 1969, when the first rocket went to the moon, Christine was around seven years old, and she dreamt of becoming an astronaut. This dream kept her focused on the US, and she was keen on learning English. In high school, Christine realized that she wasn't good enough in science to become an astronaut. She leveraged her strength in Mathematics and English to join a French Business School. She was selected for a joint MBA programme with a university in the US. Her dream to go to the US was fulfilled, but after completing her MBA, she could not find any jobs there and decided to come back to France!

In 1984, she joined a French company in Northern France. Two years later, she switched jobs to join a plant operated by Motorola in Southern France. At that time, Motorola had an internal email exchange programme through which all global teams were connected. Shortly after she joined Motorola, she came across an internal job opening in the US. With a lot of excitement in her eyes, she went to her boss to check if she could apply to that position. Her boss told her that she needed to prove herself in her current role before being considered for a job at the company headquarters in the US. She was disheartened about missing the opportunity but was motivated to prove herself.

At that time, Motorola was trying to shorten the legal books closing time from five days to one day. This was the beginning of the computer era in Europe, and she learnt computer programming to extract data from a mainframe computer database. With this new skill and her accounting background, she contributed to the development of a computer system that shortened the inventory closing time and helped Motorola finance achieve its goal.

Two years later, she was given a short-term assignment in Germany to train a team on a new finance program. Though Christine had studied German in school, she was somewhat nervous about the assignment. During this assignment, besides improving her German-speaking skills, Christine learnt about working in a different cultural environment. The cost accountants were her age, and her assignment was of only six months, so first she tried to get them to work as a team, but she found out that the Germans were expecting her to provide more direction. She had to adapt her management

Photo of Christine (extreme right) with her husband and daughter

style to become more directive with her co-workers. Christine understood that German work culture was different from French and adapted to it by providing clear directions. After this assignment, she was given the responsibility to train colleagues across the globe. She was sent to Phoenix in the US. When she landed in Phoenix, she was amazed to discover a city in the middle of the desert. It seemed so artificial to her! She liked the quiet and calm of the city and had barely had the time to find an apartment when she was off to Hong Kong to train another team. However, something in her knew that she would be back soon.

The senior leadership was impressed with her, and she was given a Controller role in Phoenix. This was a very different profile from what she had managed earlier. She learnt the skills to work with humans rather than with computers and managing business partners' expectations. These were new skills in comparison to her previous profile. Christine was enjoying her job, and her dream to work in the US was getting fulfilled. In Phoenix, at one of the international finance team events, she met a Japanese national Yasushi, who was on a one-year assignment from Motorola Japan. As two foreigners in Phoenix, they spent time together discovering Arizona. There was something in Yasushi that attracted Christine towards him, and they both fell in love. At the end of his year-long assignment, he went back to Japan, but both of them missed each other terribly. This was not the era of Facebook or WhatsApp, and the only way to stay connected was expensive international phone calls!

Managing a long-distance relationship wasn't easy. Christine used to think at times *'How will this relationship continue? Is Yasushi even serious about me?'* Then one day, in one of the phone calls, Yasushi asked Christine to take an assignment in Japan so that they could be with each other more and Christine could experience Japan's life.

Meanwhile, Yasushi talked about his relationship with Christine to Motorola Japan's CFO and requested him for help. In parallel, Christine's sponsor in the US checked with her on her next move, and she expressed interest in an assignment in Japan. Things had not really crystallized yet on job opportunities in Japan. Finally, one day Christine took the courage and booked tickets for Japan. She packed her bags and went on a personal trip to see Yasushi's world. She landed in Japan to find a country different from France and the US. She loved spending time with Yasushi and knowing him closely. One day, Yasushi informed her about a new finance manager job posting in the manufacturing plant of Motorola being set up in Northern Japan in Sendai. Christine applied for the job and appeared for an interview. And she was selected! She was the first woman in the Motorola US team to be transferred to Japan.

In Japan, most people spoke only Japanese, so it was essential for her to learn this language. She studied Japanese in night classes in the US after work. She spent the first three months in another Motorola plant in Japan while the new plant was being built. It was very tough to adjust in Japan as most of the people didn't understand English, and there were hardly any females at plants. During her stint at the existing plant in Japan, she built a great rapport with a Japanese native who was the finance manager at the plant. He was a respected leader, and the plant workers trusted him. Christine helped him improve the plant's reporting with her computer skills, and he was super impressed with her knowledge.

When the new plant was built and operational, she moved to the northern part of Japan. Amongst the 300 employees at the plant, she was the only female foreigner and manager at the young age of 29. All the other managers were Japanese males in their 40's or 50's. On day one, when Christine walked into the production floor of the newly set up plant, she looked around and could see frowning faces. The workers on the production floor raised their eyebrows and were not willing to accept a young foreign female as their manager. If any worker or team member had any query or required any help, they would refuse to reach out to Christine. Instead, they would call up the Finance Manager of another plant to discuss their issues. Christine felt bad but she didn't lose hope, nor did she try to impose her authority on workers and team members.

The good part was that Christine had built a great rapport with the other Finance Manager within the first few weeks in Japan by helping him in automating his finance reports. He would contact Christine about issues or requests shared by Christine's team on phone. Christine would then work on the solutions to the issues raised or cater to any requests her team had. Her next step used to be to get back to workers and team members with updates on how she planned to resolve their issues. This "triangle" communication continued for a year till the workers got comfortable reaching out to her directly. Christine also analyzed that she needed to break the language barrier and hence quickly learnt to speak Japanese "on the job". She did her first performance appraisal with her team after a year in Japanese. Her focus in her first year at the job was to survive and gain credibility with her team and stakeholders, and she succeeded.

She had several challenges during the first year, but she took them all head-on considering them as opportunities and came out of them successfully. In 1992, when she was comfortable that she could stay in Japan for the rest of her life, she got married to her boyfriend, Yasushi. In 1993, they had their first child, a son whom they named Georges. On the other hand, Yasushi and Christine were aware that they couldn't grow professionally if they stayed at Sendai. They decided to move to Tokyo from Sendai, and coincidentally, both got great roles in the Motorola Tokyo office reporting to the same CFO. As they moved to a new city with a baby, Christine was worried about how she would manage work and baby simultaneously.

Yasushi and Christine sat together to chalk out a plan on how they would together manage their work and home by discussing with their boss about the specific office hours and work arrangements. The good thing was that Yasushi's sister offered to babysit their son Georges when both were at work. Christine would start her day early at the office and

Photo of Christine with her son

wrap up early to pick up her son on the way back home, while her husband would take care of morning duties at home and drop his son at his sister's place on the way to the office. Both supported each other and managed work and family beautifully.

In 1996, they had their second child, a daughter whom they named Mari. They made sure that the names of their kids could be pronounced both in French and Japanese. Meanwhile, Yasushi wanted to pursue an MBA from the United States to grow in his career. Christine's boss helped her find an Internal Controls manager role in Phoenix. For two years in Phoenix, while Christine was at work, Yasushi would take care of the kids at home as he had shorter hours at the university.

In 1998, they moved back to Japan. Christine's boss again was of great support and helped her find a job at Motorola Japan, but her husband decided to join another company in Japan as they didn't want to be co-workers anymore.

By the year 2000, Christine had done multiple finance roles in Motorola, and she decided that this was the right time in her career to explore CFO profiles outside Motorola. At that time, there was no LinkedIn or other internet-based job portals in Japan. She went to the French Chamber of Commerce in Japan and got her name registered for any CFO opening with French companies!

A year later, in 2001, the French Chamber of Commerce informed her that a French Global Company was looking for a CFO in their Japan office in Tokyo. After 15 years at Motorola, Christine joined BioMerieux, a medical device company, as CFO, and her assignment was to establish financial controls within the organization. Three months later, Yasushi was transferred to Kobe city in Japan. Given that Christine had just joined the new company, Yasushi moved alone to Kobe. Christine struggled to manage her new job and two kids all by herself in Tokyo. She had to reluctantly quit her job within a year and relocate with her family to Kobe city.

Christine tried to find a job in Kobe, but Kobe was a smaller city and she failed to find any suitable job. She was very sad for a few weeks over her failed attempts. Then one day she decided that instead of being dejected, she would enjoy the current moments with her kids and be at home. The first few weeks weren't easy as she had always lived a busy corporate life. But after a few weeks, she started loving being with the kids and watching them grow. She cherished this time off and enjoyed every moment with her children. Meanwhile, with a lot of time on hand, she decided to learn how to read and write in the Japanese language and also cleared the formal exams of the language. She knew these skills would help her in the future when they moved back to Tokyo.

Finally, they moved back to Tokyo, and after the children joined their new schools, Christine decided that it was time to get back to work. Coincidentally she received a call from BioMerieux asking her to join back as CFO. In three years, her role was expanded to include Human Resources, Infrastructure and Technology support, and logistics functions.

In 2007, the French Chamber of Commerce contacted her again and informed her about an opening in a French baby clothing retail group planning to expand its presence in Japan. In April 2007, she joined this group to set up their finance, HR, ITS, and logistics functions. She worked to implement ERP and re-organized logistics and warehouses with adequate inventory controls. She also seconded the General Manager to create new stores. The management wanted the team to open the first flagship store at a very good location at Omotesando, a premium upscale area. The team applied for rented space in a building that was owned by an association of Nurses. Christine and the team knew that given the budget limitations; it wouldn't be easy to win the deal. The association of Nurses called all the applicants to present their pitch and financial proposal. Christine came up with an idea along with her team that they will carry the actual baby cloth samples and try to convince the nurses explaining to them the benefits of having high-quality baby clothing chain stores in Japan. Their idea worked, and they opened their first flagship store at Omotesando.

The best part of this team was that it majorly consisted of women, which was very unusual in Japan. Most of the team members were young single Japanese women, and Christine attended many colleagues' marriages, and baby showers function during her five years stint in this company. Christine was also tasked to build the financial infrastructure for the company. Again, it wasn't an easy task as the company couldn't afford big ERP systems like SAP or Oracle. She met multiple vendors but wasn't comfortable with the level of customization required for their company. One day she came across an advertisement in the newspaper of a Japanese company with Microsoft-based ERP. This company was recently inherited by a passionate and aspirational young female from her father. When Christine and her team met them for a demo, they came up with a solution to fit their needs and budget. The ERP was successfully implemented, and Christine feels so proud of her choice even years later.

In the year 2015, she was approached by Sanofi, a leading multinational pharma company, to join them as Head of Controlling. Though it wasn't a CFO position, Christine took this opportunity. A year later, this role disappeared due to organizational changes in the company, and she was offered the position of Business Unit Controller. While Christine was having second thoughts on whether she should stay with the company, she was assigned to a special project by the CFO in addition to her day job. She was given the task of reducing real estate costs by 20% by implementing activity-based seating arrangements. Christine successfully managed this project and felt that dealing with the emotions of the colleagues during the change management period was the most challenging thing she had to do on this project.

The headquarters and the senior management team were particularly impressed with Christine's work, and she was rewarded for her hard work by being promoted as Asia Facilities Manager. She successfully managed similar projects across other offices in Asia.

In the year 2019, Christine expressed her interest to return to Finance. She was granted her wish in the same year when she was offered the position of CFO in the Korean market. This was to be an 18 months assignment with the key responsibility to go to Korea and groom a top talent for the CFO position. During this time, Yasushi had just retired, and George and Mari started working in corporate jobs in Tokyo. She decided to move to Korea alone to keep it less disruptive for the family, and she could travel back home easily on weekends. She enjoyed the experience of interacting with the people in Korea and understanding their culture, which was very different from the Japanese culture.

While her first challenge was to transfer the accounting team to an internal shared service centre, she focused on building a solid team and teaching her new team the importance of teamwork. However, in early 2020 when the COVID-19 crisis erupted, with travel restrictions, she could not meet her family until November 2020. This was a particularly difficult time for the entire family. Meanwhile, when her 18-month assignment ended, she went back to another finance role in Tokyo.

Christine started her career 37 years back and is proud to have earned respect as a finance professional with illustrious international experience.

Christine's leadership mantras are:

- Develop and groom a strong team.
- Collaboration is the key in the workplace to be successful.
- Take calculated risks and challenges to grow in your career—find the right balance between career and family. Working in diverse roles and diverse culture is helpful in a career in the long run.

CHAPTER 6

Being Comfortable in Being Out of the Comfort Zone

This is a story about a woman who for 33 long years believed that her world was limited to the small industrial city of Taubate, a traditional city located in South-eastern Brazil. It was her own fears and thoughts that kept her back from venturing out and exploring the world and herself.

And the way she blossomed when she ventured out of her comfort zone! She went on to become the first female CFO of a multinational company in Brazil's largest metropolitan city. And when she was getting comfortable there, having spent 20 years in the Power and Infrastructure Industry, she again took a leap and moved to the Food Industry to reinvent herself. Today, she is a happier and more confident person, having enjoyed different experiences in life.

Let me introduce you to Jamile Aun. She is a simple, middle-aged, down-to-earth woman. She has excitement in her voice when you speak to her about her recent career move as a CFO in a global company in Food Industry. She is the mother of a teenage daughter. She is currently working in the metropolitan city, São Paulo, in Brazil, and she misses the calmness and serenity of her hometown Taubate. She travels back every weekend to her hometown where her family lives.

As Jamile was growing up in school, the city also grew as an industrial centre with several companies setting up their

Photo of Jamile with her daughter and husband

manufacturing plants, including companies like Volkswagen, Alstom, Ford, LG, and Embraer, amongst many others.

She grew up as a kid in the 1970's era with no computers and mobile phones. She loved playing simulation games of money and cheques instead of playing with her dolls as a child. So much so that she once actually sold her dolls to her father, Jorge, in exchange for real money. As a child, she remembers the feeling of satisfaction and success she felt when she did this. She felt independent and capable of earning money all by herself. With the money she earned, she asked her mother if she could buy dresses for herself. Her mother hugged her and gave her permission with a smile. Jamile loves shopping for clothes even today. Now, she and her daughter, Sophia, go out together on weekends to shop. In childhood, she loved numbers and data analysis and never liked subjects like biology or chemistry. Jamile, being a sensitive human by nature, felt uncomfortable even imagining the sufferings of a human being. She was always happy dealing with numbers, documents, and papers as these had no feelings or emotions. As a teenager, she made up her mind to take up finance as a career and work in a multinational company in her city where she wanted to spend her entire life.

Jamile completed her graduation in accounting and master's in business administration (MBA) from the University of Taubate. Taubate is also a university city. The University of Taubate, UNITAU, attracts young people from all over the country who come to study in one of its many colleges. In the year 1994, she joined the Alstom Hydroelectric factory in Taubate in the finance team. She was the youngest and only female in her team.

After 9 months as a trainee, Jamile was moved to a new permanent position sponsored by the Finance Director in the company. When she met her male manager, he told her, "I don't like working with women, and I had a bad experience in the past with a woman subordinate." It wasn't motivating to hear such words from her boss on her first day at the job, but Jamile being rebellious by nature, took this as a challenge. Her boss was a married man and had specifically instructed her not to pick and answer his office phone. She wondered if his wife was even aware about presence of female colleague in the office! Once, Jamile had gone to a supermart with her father Jorge for shopping on the weekend. Her boss, along with his wife, was also shopping at the same supermart. She told Jorge, pointing out at the couple that they were her boss and his wife. Taubate being a small city, Jorge knew the boss's wife well. Jorge insisted Jamile go and visit the couple. Jamile was hesitant initially, but her father took her along and greeted the couple. Jorge introduced Jamile to her boss's wife, and she was happy to know that she was Jorge's daughter. After this instance, Jamile's equation with her boss improved significantly at work.

At work, Jamile's team comprised of five other team members who were all men in the age group of 40 to 50 years. They were all very capable and intelligent but were just waiting for their retirement. From their outlook on life and work, she realized that life is a long journey, and one needs to keep oneself motivated. Jamile loved her job and was super motivated. She worked almost 17 hours a day in the early years of her career. Being a white-collared employee in a factory, she was expected to be disciplined and learnt early in her career how to create a positive environment for employees on the shop floor. When Jamile first visited the shop floor area in the factory, the worker thought that the young lady was a visitor. For the first few weeks when she would visit the shop floor, all eyes were on her as they had never seen a young female in the factory premises. In those times, most females chose to work at banks or schools. They were surprised to see how passionate Jamile was about the production parameters on the shop floor and would take a keen interest to increase productivity. After a few months, the workers felt comfortable sharing their concerns with Jamile and contributing to improving productivity. She listened to them attentively and tried to solve their concerns by bringing those up with the senior leaders.

Hardworking Jamile was a quick learner. She learnt about the company's business, industry factors and was able to connect the dots of finance numbers with ease. As the Brazilian economy grew in the 1990s, the manufacturing units were also growing with international export orders. Jamile grew in her career, taking on more responsibilities managing exports related reporting and compliances. Portuguese is the most spoken language in Brazil. Jamile had the edge over others as she had excellent English communication skills. She was promoted and was responsible for the consolidation of financial results for the entire Latin American region. This role provided her with the opportunity to work with global finance teams and senior leadership at Alstom's Headquarters in Paris.

At the age of 27, she was promoted as a Controller for the Water Division at Alstom. She had a team of 15 people to manage. This was her first experience as a people manager. Jamile felt honoured by her promotion, but this transition from an individual contributor role to a people manager with higher responsibilities wasn't easy. Within a few days in this new role, Jamile started feeling restless as she felt she wasn't aware of all details and was responsible for work done by others. She was also a perfectionist and expected the same delivery standards from her team members. They felt she was arrogant, aggressive, and demanding as a boss. Jamile soon realized that to succeed, she needed to get out of her comfort zone and needed to groom and trust her team instead of being a control freak. It wasn't easy to change. She learnt each day from her mistakes and experimented with different ideas to become a strong leader and form a great team. In this role, she was responsible for cash collections from the clients. This was also the first experience for her where she had to deal with people outside her company. She went to meet one of the clients of the company and was promised payment of funds within five days. She was very happy as the timely receipt of money would help manage the cashflows for the next week. She duly informed the CFO of this favourable outcome. Unfortunately, the client called her on the promised date of payment that funds were not available and will be available after a few days. She was distraught and felt terrible to inform her CFO about being unable to meet her commitment. Jamile soon realized that this was a common pattern from her clients, and she learnt the hard way how to manage and plan for cashflows in such an uncertain environment.

After three years in this role, the Divisional Controller roles were eliminated in the company due to restructuring. Jamile's strong leadership skills were noticed by the senior manager, and she was made the Group Controller. She was made responsible for standardizing the controls and processes across all divisions. This was the first opportunity for her to assist change management on a large scale, and that helped her strengthen her influencing skills.

Two years later, Jamile had to choose between the options to either continue as Controller or to move to the Tax team or to set up a Project Management Office (PMO) for her company from scratch. As the company was growing at a fast pace, the new PMO team was supposed to set up new controls and train business units on risk mitigation, contract penalties, foreign exchange exposures and government regulations.

She decided to try out something new. Jamile decided to take on the challenge to set up the PMO team. She started with a team of 4 and grew it up to 45 folks. She worked with different project teams, studied contracts clauses, regulations of customer countries, identified risks and set up controls. She groomed talent for control monitoring and review activities. Such talent wasn't readily available in the market. This was also a very interesting phase in Brazil's economy, and the manufacturing sector was growing fast. Other manufacturing companies also soon realized the need to set up control teams in their organization. As a result, Jamile started losing talent in her team to competitors who were offering a minimum 30-40% pay hike. This was the first time ever in her career that she had to put on her goals, people retention as an agenda. She collaborated with the Human Resources team to analyze

Photo of Jamile

the market pay parity data, created retention packages and strategies for long-term engagement. At the same time, she realized that some people that she groomed deserved better in life. While being a manager, she couldn't display her emotions openly, but she felt happy and proud when any of her team members got a great opportunity outside, which she couldn't have offered. She strongly believes that at times for the betterment of someone, you must let them go and grow.

Jamile was growing and enjoying her career in Taubate. On the personal front, she also found her life partner, Sergio, in this city. She got married and started her family. She was blessed with a baby girl, Sophia, and everything in her life was going well. She had the full support of her parents, which helped her manage her professional life along with personal family commitments. During this period, she declined two fantastic career opportunities to work at Alstom Headquarters in Paris. The excuse she provided when rejecting these job offers was that her husband wouldn't move from Brazil. Deep in her heart, she knew this was not the case, and her husband was always willing to relocate and explore new cities and places. The fear of leaving her small city and moving to a new place was holding her back.

At the age of 33 years, she was offered an opportunity as a Regional Latin America Controller, but this position was based out of São Paulo main city, around 160km away from Taubate. This time, she took a lot of courage and took a lifetime decision to move to a metropolitan city. Her husband and her parents backed her decision and provided her confidence that she will be successful with their support. Jamile decided to move to São Paulo without her family, with plans to travel back on weekends. Sophia was just five years old then. The fact that Jamile's mother agreed to live with Sophia during weekdays was a big relief for her. She immediately hired a nanny whom she could trust for Sophia and even found the right playschool in Taubate for Sophia. She and her family adapted to this new normal soon. Sophia grew up as a responsible kid; she would know what things she could do with her father and grandmother during weekdays and what to leave for weekends Jamile still misses being part of her daughter's school functions during weekdays. Sophia is now around 15 years old, a mature, responsible girl, and very supportive of her Mom's career. Sophia stays in touch with Jamile through technology like WhatsApp, emails and phone during weekdays.

At the work front, as a regional controller, 50% of her time was involved in travelling within Latin America. Jamile had butterflies in her stomach when she boarded her first international flight after becoming a mother, and she watched the ocean beneath her from her flight. She was worried about her life insurance in case something was to happen to the aircraft.

She proved herself again at work in a new environment, and within a year, she was promoted as the CFO for the Latin America region for Alstom Grid Group. She was the first woman and first Brazilian to hold the CFO position. She managed multiple finance functions together as part of this profile. In four years, she spearheaded some crucial mergers and acquisitions for Alstom, including the acquisition of Alstom power units by GE in Power and Grid business for Latin America, a very complex M&A involving cultural changes and transformation.

In the year 2016, Jamile got an opportunity to work outside Alstom, which she thought would help her diversify her "portfolio". It was not a CFO position but as Director of Finance and Technology in a subsidiary of an American Publishing company. After 20 years in the Power Industry in one company, Jamile took the courage to get out of her comfort zone and join a new Industry. Meanwhile, she also completed her MBA Advanced Boardroom programme. She aimed to be better prepared for new experiences in the boardrooms of Brazilian companies, with a special focus on Governance and Compliance.

Two years later, she was offered the role of VP Finance Latin America region at Alstom Transportation company. Many of the mentors and friends told her that since she had already worked at Alstom for 20 years, she wouldn't learn anything new by joining the group. They were wrong as the Transport Industry is very different from the Power Industry. Infrastructure and especially transport was growing at a fast pace during this time in Latin America, especially in countries like Panama, Mexico, and Chile.

At that stage in her life, Jamile was conscious that none of her profiles gave her the opportunity to interact directly with end consumers of the services or products of the company she served.

With this in mind, she joined as the CFO at Gomes da Costa (Calvo Group), a global food company specialized in canned fish and seafood. This was a very different industry from power and transport. In the Power Industry, while everyone uses energy, the end consumer never cares about how energy is being created as long as they have an uninterrupted supply. But in the food industry, the end consumers have feelings attached to the food they eat. They always have suggestions on even minute details like packing, new flavour, and source of the food. The canned food industry grew during the 2020 pandemic as people started eating at home. She created working capital and long-term capital strategies for the company to manage the growth and promote innovation.

One learning which made Jamile successful was that she learnt the importance of having complementing skills in the team with diverse perspectives to make it complete. She focused on how she could create a strong team with folks complementing her and each other on technical and soft skills. These learnings at a young age helped her later in her career to take tough decisions on layoffs much more objectively and rationally without any bias. Once she faced a situation to lay off some of her team members, which wasn't easy. For a few days, she had sleepless nights and then she learnt that she needed to separate her emotions from the task assigned to her. As a leader, one must act in the best interests of the company.

Jamile has been consciously carrying out self-assessment at every phase in her career to understand what she needs to add to her experience to become a well-rounded professional. She has also focused on grooming talent in her team and leaving a strong legacy behind when she moves out, pursuing new challenges. Conscious of her responsibility towards the future women leaders, Jamile, together with other talented Women CFOs recently created an organization to sponsor and develop a pipeline for female leadership and promote a strong network. Today, Jamile is also a very active part of initiatives and not-for-profit organizations that work for Brazil's communities.

Today, Jamile describes herself as not perfect, but happy, independent, and a little stressed but a very confident, self-made woman.

Jamile's Leadership mantras are:

- When under pressure, keep calm to take the best decisions.

- Do not be afraid of change.

- Be a learner in life. You never stop learning because life never stops teaching.

- The best way to predict the future is to create it.

CHAPTER 7

If I Can, You Can

Sandhya's father, Ram Karan, loved her a lot. One day, Ram was shocked to learn that his close friend's daughter had eloped with a guy from a different caste. Ram was heartbroken to see this. In a knee jerk reaction to this, Ram found a suitable match for Sandhya in a hurry and wanted her to get married, even though her graduation was not completed. Sandhya was almost in tears as she wanted to study. She told her mother, "I don't want to get married!!" After much deliberation, Sandhya got married at the age of 20. Read ahead for the story of Sandhya, who had the willpower and the perseverance to break the glass ceiling and become the CFO of a multinational company despite getting married at a very young age.

Sandhya's parents belong to the state of Bihar in India and were married when her mother was only 14 years old. Her mother, Rajkali, couldn't complete her studies beyond the 4th standard. Her father, Ram Karan, continued to study after marriage and completed his textile engineering. The family subsequently moved to Mumbai, where Ram Karan worked in the textile industry as production in charge.

Sandhya was born after 13 years of her parents' marriage. Just like any other loving father, her father loved and pampered Sandhya, but her grandmother always frowned on having a granddaughter. She wanted a grandson instead. When Ram Karan would hug Sandhya, his mother would taunt him and say, "What's the use of loving a girl child so much,

Photo of Sandhya

who can't even do your last rites when you die? A girl child is just a burden and nothing more than that!!"

In Hindu tradition, only the son can do the last rites of the parents, and a girl child doesn't have this right. However, in current times, this tradition has been broken by many families in India, but 50 years ago, it was beyond anyone's imagination. Ram Karan was not affected by his mother's taunts and loved Sandhya unconditionally.

Sandhya's upbringing in a middle-class family with limited resources and humble background taught her many life lessons, which she replicated at her workplace while handling the year 2020 pandemic crisis. Sandhya used to stay in a crowded colony of middle-class families in Mumbai. It was common for many of her neighbours to visit her house and share their family problems with her mother about their kids not focusing on studies, issues they were facing with their husband or challenges in managing household expenses. Sandhya watched how her mother Rajkali would empathetically listen to their problems and share her thoughts on how to resolve the issues with a positive attitude. Rajkali was a great cook and would generously share homemade evening snacks with the visitors. Rajkali had limited resources, but she planned the family finances very well to ensure good food and good clothes for her family while cutting down on unnecessary expenses.

During the pandemic of 2020, when Sandhya faced a cash crisis in her company, she replicated the same learnings. She analyzed the financial health of her customers to ask for early payment release from those who were financially strong and offered extra credit periods to those struggling. On the other hand, she released money to the vendors who were struggling to stay afloat. She ensured adequate cash is available to pay salaries to staff and froze the discretionary spending.

Sandhya's parents never had too many expectations from her, and she was an average student in academics. She had a happy childhood with few close friends. She had a brother, Manoj, seven years younger than her, who always looked upon her as a caring elder sister. Interestingly, Rajkali named her son Manoj as she was a great fan of Indian cinema actor Manoj Kumar. Manoj always followed Sandhya everywhere, even to birthday parties of her friends and even tagged along with her to movie outings with her friends. Sandhya's friends also loved and pampered Manoj as a younger brother. Sandhya enjoyed his company and was never really irritated that he was always tagging along with her.

In her 10th grade, Sandhya selected commerce stream by sheer elimination and did not have any big plans for the future. She was just cautious not to choose Arts stream as she always got feedback of bad handwriting, which she thought is a sign of not being creative!!

While she was studying her graduation course, she had the realization that she wanted to do something in life and make a professional career for herself. She wanted to be financially independent. The words of her father in the Hindi language, *"kama ke koi nahi deta" (No one will earn money for you)*, had a big impact on her. But life had different plans for her. Sandhya's father found a suitable match for her and wanted her to get married. One Sunday, Ram Karan and Rajkali discussed with Sandhya that Shyam whom she had met as a relative earlier, was being considered as a probable match for her. Sandhya was almost in tears, and she wanted to study; she told her mother, "I don't want to get married!!" Rajkali told her, "Think about it for a few days; we are in no hurry, also think what future plans you have for yourself and would marriage stop them?" Sandhya was determined that she would never break her parents' hearts. She also thought about her future and felt that she should speak openly to Shyam to let him know that she wanted to pursue studies after marriage. Sandhya met Shyam and found out that he was very supportive of her idea to continue her studies. Sandhya went back to her mother and told her, "I am fine to get married to Shyam, please start making the arrangements."

Sandhya got married at the age of 20. She continued with her studies after marriage. Once she got her graduation degree, the big question playing on her mind was *'What's next?'*

One weekend, Shyam's cousin Shiv Kumar joined them for evening tea and snacks, and he suggested to Sandhya, "Why don't you enrol yourself for Chartered Accountancy (CA) professional course?"

Sandhya's reaction was, "Oh! I have heard that course is very difficult!"

"Sandhya, you are a very bright lady, and I believe you are capable of doing this course," reassured Shiv. Shyam agreed with Shiv and added, "Sandhya, you have the potential, and you should give it a thought, and I am always here to back you."

Next weekend Sandhya visited her parents to hear their views on the CA course and voiced her concerns on how could she manage tough studies along with household responsibilities. Rajkali offered to cook food for Sandhya and Shyam, while Ram Karan offered to provide any other support if required.

However, the constant support behind her was Shyam, who not only shouldered the responsibility to cook and take care of the house but was positive support during the difficult times of managing articleship and studies.

Motivated by family members, Sandhya enrolled in the course. She joined a CA firm for internship training and continued her studies. Sandhya cleared the intermediate CA exams and was all set with her preparations for the final CA exams. Just two days before the exams, Sandhya and Shyam received a phone call informing them of the untimely death of Shiv Kumar. Sandhya was in a state of shock hearing this news; it felt as if someone had pulled the earth beneath her feet. Shyam and Sandhya rushed to meet Shiv's family to support the family. Sandhya was in grief and wasn't even in the state of mind to appear for her exams. It took her almost a month to get outside of this shock. She was shattered and couldn't reconcile to the fact that Shiv, who motivated her to enrol for CA exams, was no longer alive. Then she questioned herself, '*What would give peace to Shiv's soul, getting a CA degree or leaving the course?*' She got her answers that had Shiv been alive, he would be proud to see a CA degree in her hands. Now, Sandhya was determined to give her best in the upcoming exams, and she cleared the exams with flying colours.

Sandhya joined "Bombay Dyeing", an Indian listed company, in the finance department and was fortunate to have a woman leader, Gayatri Panicker, as her department head. Gayatri was a strong personality with excellent accounting skills that inspired Sandhya each day. One lesson that Gayatri taught Sandhya was that in case of conflicts, focus on facts rather than the incident. Gayatri shared one real-life story with Sandhya. "As Internal Audit Head, one day I went to the cabin of the Production Head who was a very senior leader in the company. I greeted him and shared the printed internal audit report findings with him. He took the report and tore it into pieces, and told me, "Look, Gayatri, I know my processes very well, and I don't want someone in finance to tell me how I need to run my production shop floor. Now, please leave the room.""

Sandhya was shocked listening to Gayatri and questioned, "What did you do then? You must have gone out and complained about his behaviour to your leaders?"

Gayatri said, "No, I didn't complain; rather, I went to my cabin and printed the report again. After that, I went again to his cabin and left the report on the table. I told him, 'Sir, when you get time, do go through the report and let me know if you have questions about my findings.'"

Sandhya asked Gayatri, "So, what was his reaction?"

Gayatri said, "I think he felt embarrassed over his actions and realized that he couldn't argue with me on factual statements. He needs to reply on the findings."

Working with a great leader in these formidable early years and opportunities like handling diverse finance roles laid a strong foundation for her.

As part of her job, Sandhya often used to visit the production line in the textile plant. On her first visit, she realized that the noise made by machines had very high decibels levels. One couldn't hear another person standing nearby unless the voice pitch is high. She could now relate to why her father had a high pitch voice. He was the production line in charge, and if he wanted to convey a message to anyone on the shop floor, he had to practically yell!

In those days, due to lack of safety measures, accidents caused some workers to lose a finger or a hand while working. Once when Sandhya witnessed such an accident in front of her, she got shocked to the core and realized how difficult it must be for her father to work on the shop floor each day, but he never showed his work stress to his kids at home. Sandhya's respect for her father increased manifold after working in the textile industry.

After a few years, she made a career move to the finance department of "Mahindra", another giant listed company in India. It allowed her to gain business knowledge about diverse industries in the Mahindra group. During her stint at Mahindra, she was blessed with a beautiful girl, Sunidhi. After three months of Sunidhi's birth, Sandhya had to join back office, but she had no support system in Mumbai as her parents had moved to a town called Kolhapur in India. Sandhya couldn't trust the daycare centre that she could afford. On the other hand, she couldn't leave her job given the financial obligations she and Shyam had. Finally, both agreed to leave Sunidhi with Rajkali in Kolhapur until she started speaking and could express herself. With a very heavy heart, Sandhya dropped Sunidhi with her Nani. While Sandhya knew that her daughter was in the best care, she lived with guilt each day without her baby. Kolhapur was an overnight train journey from Mumbai, so Sandhya travelled every fortnight to Kolhapur to spend the weekend with Sunidhi and would come back to Mumbai early Monday. She would make phone calls every day just to hear Sunidhi's voice. On Fridays, when she had to travel to Kolhapur, Sandhya would complete all the office tasks by checking in early during the day to leave the office by 5 pm. Saturday mornings for Sunidhi were the best time as she would wake up early to meet her mom and play with her. Rajkali played a pivotal role during the three years when Sunidhi stayed with her. Sandhya consciously made a personal choice to focus on her career, as she didn't want to take special privileges at work being a mother.

Once Sunidhi turned three years old, Sandhya and Shyam brought her back to Mumbai and hired a nanny to help her manage the house. This arrangement allowed Sandhya to concentrate on work and spend time with her daughter whenever possible. This phase of her life wasn't easy; she had stretched work hours and would return home late every night. Sunidhi would go to birthday parties of her school friends accompanied by her nanny while most of her friends had their mothers accompanying them. Soon, Sunidhi realized that Sandhya is a working professional; it is not feasible for her to accompany her.

Once, Sunidhi went to a friend's birthday party and liked the arrangements. Back from the party, she called up Sandhya at the office with a lot of excitement and said, "Mummy, I just came from a birthday party and the arrangement was awesome. I want to share that with you." Sandhya had to interrupt her as she was in the middle of a meeting with her team and suggested that she would listen to her once back at home. That night Sandhya returned home late at night, around 10 pm. Sandhya entered Sunidhi's room and found her sleeping. Sandhya broke down, and tears started rolling down her cheeks. She felt sad as she knew this was not just a one-off incidence but was now a regular feature in their lives. At that point in time of her life, Sandhya was on the very verge of giving up, and she thought of taking a career break to spend time with her daughter.

But her destiny had something else planned for her; she got an interview call from Schindler India Private Limited, which offered her a profile with reasonable working hours and weekend offs that allowed her to spend quality time with her family. As Sandhya started spending more time with Sunidhi, she realized that Sunidhi not only wanted to share what's happening in her school or with friends but wanted guidance and help from her mom, which Sandhya wasn't doing justice to earlier. Sandhya soon found out that Sunidhi had been grappling with bullying at school by one of her classmates. Sandhya went to Sunidhi's school to discuss this issue with her teachers and got to know that the student bullying Sunidhi was a special child, and she wasn't doing it purposefully with Sunidhi.

Sandhya came back from school and sat with Sunidhi. Sandhya said, "Baby, I know you have gone through a lot, and you are very upset. But do you know that the one who is bullying you is not doing it purposefully; she is a special child. We are privileged that God made us normal, but she is not. I want you to be empathetic to her and try to ignore if you feel she is troubling you." Sunidhi discussed each day how she handled her classmate's comments and would hear Sandhya's thoughts. In a matter of a few months, Sunidhi was a very happy and confident girl. Today, Sunidhi is in college, and Sandhya is her best friend. She shares a special bond with Sandhya, and there are no secrets between them. They watch movies and web series together and also go shopping occasionally. Sunidhi shares her feelings and even gossips about boyfriends with her mom. Sandhya has given complete independence to her daughter and has never imposed her expectations on Sunidhi. In these years, Sandhya could nurture her daughter and make gradual progression in her career at Schindler and was elevated to be appointed as their CFO.

Her optimistic attitude towards life and the powerful backing of her husband at home helped her approach work with a positive attitude every single day. There were moments when she had some team members who she could make out didn't like her a lot. Sandhya introspected in such situations and made sure that she didn't let her biases impact her actions when dealing with such people. She started experimenting with ways to solve this problem by having candid one-on-one discussions with such team members.

In these discussions, Sandhya ensured that her entire focus was on the individual to understand what expectations they had. She avoided topics like *'What she or the company expected from the team member!'* Usually, after the meetings, individuals would self-reflect upon their strengths and identify what makes them happy and what they want to do in their careers. The next discussion would then be more meaningful and healthier. This helped her distinguish herself as a trusted leader at work. She would then make conscious efforts to help each of them by assigning a mentor or coach and helped colleagues move to other departments like sales or administration to deliver their best and rise fast in their careers. In this way, she could bring happiness to someone's life at work. This not only gave her satisfaction at work but also helped her in getting selected as the CFO at Schindler.

Sandhya has always been focused on great customer experience in her dealings. Once, Sandhya was on a call with a customer who hadn't paid his dues for the past six months due to a financial crisis. Sandhya had two options—the first one was to file a legal case against the customer to recover the dues, and the second was to discuss with the customer what help she could render to help them come out of the crisis and complete the project so that they could pay back the dues. Sandhya chose the second option as she knew that a customer once lost is lost for a lifetime. She signed a triparty arrangement with the customer and banker after approval from the leadership team. A year later, the customer paid back all their dues, and their relationship strengthened to get more orders later.

During her professional journey to the CFO position, there were some life instances that taught her life lessons and made her more determined to succeed. Early in her career, the untimely death of her colleague who left his widow and kids behind with no money taught her how critical it is for any female to be financially independent and be actively involved in the family's financial planning.

In the year 2020, the pandemic taught her a lot. It was one of the best years in her career, and her humble middle-class upbringing lessons helped her manage company finances in critical times. She learnt how the CFO could partner with the business and shift from the role of "lead and load" to "lead and share the load". The ability to trust business partners helped her sail through the 2020 crisis.

Sandhya as a person is full of gratitude towards life. She feels blessed that not only did she get the opportunity to complete her studies post marriage, but also got great family support to achieve a fulfilling career. She feels humbled that her parents' values helped her decide what is right or wrong and always act with integrity. Over the past few years, Sandhya has been making conscious efforts to share her life stories with others to inspire many young female professionals to be independent. She is vocal about the menopause phase which she is currently going through in her life. She strongly feels the need to create more awareness on this topic as male family members and colleagues at the workplace can be more empathetic to women. She strongly believes that more and more CFOs have the potential to become CEOs in the future.

Sandhya's leadership mantras are:

- As a finance professional, understand the company's business extremely well.

- Know your internal and external customers well.

- Develop an excellent team.

- Pay it forward – Get involved in social service activities.

- Have your spiritual path – know the capabilities of your mind.

- Manage your personal and mental health to stay calm and stress-free.

CHAPTER 8

Trying to Fit In

A girl born in a small town in India always attempted to adapt and fit into the various situations that have come her way, starting from boarding school environment as a nine-year-old girl to moving across three continents and adapting to different cultures and cities. She has been a big supporter of minority group rights; she participated in the South African movement against racism and, at the workplace, ensured that females also have the right to wear trousers instead of only skirts in chilling cold weather. She later stormed her way to CFO and COO positions in a male-dominated Hedge Fund Industry in the United Kingdom. During the year 2020, she joined Testing for All (TFA), a not-for-profit organization set up with a mission to help in the COVID-19 pandemic by providing affordable, mass testing services for COVID-19 in the UK.

Alka Sharma was born in Dehradun in India. Her parents always wanted the best education for their daughters and wanted them to be independent. Her father is a finance professional, and her mother is a homemaker. Alka's parents moved from India to Zambia in Africa in 1974. Her father was appointed as Gaborone City Treasurer by Botswana Finance Ministry. At the age of nine, she and her younger sister were sent from Zambia to Welham Girls' School, a very reputed and top private boarding school for girls located in Dehradun, India. The school was home to many girls from very affluent families. Though Alka's parents were from a well-to-do professional family, they were not amongst the wealthiest,

Photo of Alka (2nd from extreme right) with her family at family function

and consciously saved and made compromises to ensure that their daughters could study in India's best institutes and overseas for their college education.

She studied in Welham for the next eight years. Her school friends were like family; they all were always there to cheer each other during good times and support each other during difficult times. During these years in school, she had developed many close bonds and made some great, lifelong friendships that she cherishes and maintains even today. At Welham's, since she couldn't read or write Hindi, she was given special classes to bring her up to speed. She felt awkward and embarrassed with all this attention. But after a few months, she adjusted well and began loving her boarding school, and even got the highest grades in Hindi in her class for the 10th board exams.

Every month during the short school breaks, Alka's maternal uncle and aunt, who were her local guardians in Dehradun, would bring her to their home. They always made her feel at home and treated her and her sister as their children in addition to their own three kids. Growing up in boarding school and away from her parents, Alka realized from a young age the importance of being part of the wider community and sharing resources with those beyond her immediate family. This upbringing made Alka realize the importance of relationships, friends, and family in both her personal life and also when she joined the corporate world. At work, she has made friends with colleagues, led teams with empathy, and built strong work relationships.

Alka loved reading and always had a book with her. At night when hostel or home lights were out, she would read her book under the blanket in the torchlight. She is still an avid reader and spends as much time as she can reading. Books have been a key part of her path of self-growth and development.

When she was in boarding school, the only way to communicate with her parents in Botswana was by letters. She would write weekly letters to her mother with details about her week at school and eagerly wait for the regular letters from her mum. Alka's mum would also include notes, scribbling, or drawings made by her two younger sisters, which Alka loved as they gave her a glimpse of how her siblings were growing up. Alka's father's letters were usually to provide practical information like flight and train details, bank information, etc. Alka would usually see her parents only once or twice a year during the school holidays when she and her two sisters as minors would travel to Delhi airport to take connecting flights to Botswana as there were no direct flights. Such experiences made Alka independent at a young age, and today as a mother to a teenage girl, she encourages her daughter to be independent much the same way her parents did.

Once Alka completed her schooling, her parents wanted her to move to Botswana for college so that they could spend some years together. Alka moved to Botswana, which was culturally very different from India. Her parents were expats in Africa and were considered foreigners. She joined the

University of Botswana to do a degree in BCom (with a double major in accounting and management studies). The University had kids from Botswana as well as a sizeable number of students from other African countries, and she was amongst the few minority students with an Asian background. Again, Alka felt she was the odd one out, but like before, she made a concerted effort and assimilated quickly. Her close group of friends was very diverse, consisting of people from Botswana, Uganda, Tanzania, and South Africa.

Interestingly most of the students, particularly those doing BCom in the university, were in their mid-20s as they generally joined after a few years of work experience. Alka was amongst the youngest students in her batch. Her friends from different backgrounds and age groups helped her understand, appreciate, and embrace diversity and helped her look at different perspectives from early in her life.

In the late '80s/early '90s, the African National Congress that was fighting against apartheid in South Africa was a very active part of the student body. Alka would join events and protests to support this movement along with other local students in Botswana despite not having her parents' permission. She got the opportunity to see Nelson Mandela and hear him speak when he visited Botswana. This was truly a unique, momentous experience, and very inspirational, and it's as clear in her mind as if it happened recently. The three years in Botswana gave Alka a unique perspective and awareness about racism and equality issues. She understood what it feels like to be a part of a minority and to stand up for your rights. When she joined the corporate world in London a few years later, the women in the office were not allowed to wear trouser suits but only skirt suits when at client sites. This was especially tough in the harsh winters when the temperatures could be below freezing. There were only a handful of women on the team, and they had never raised this matter. Alka spoke to the other women and spoke to the senior leadership in her team to allow women to wear trousers. Her experience in Botswana helped her stand up for simple inequalities at the workplace, which, if raised and put forward logically, were supported by all.

After graduating from the University of Botswana, Alka was deliberating on her next move for further studies. She was very keen to study in the US and wanted to apply for an MBA course, but most courses require at least two years of work experience. Her professor guided her to do the Chartered Accountancy qualification from the Institute of Chartered Accountants in England and Wales (UK ACA). This would provide her with corporate work experience for the MBA while she worked as a trainee accountant in one of the Big 4 accountancy firms in the UK and also provide financial independence.

Alka applied for an internship at some of the major accounting firms in London and went there for two weeks for interviews. This was the first time she had travelled to Europe. She got internship offers from many firms that she interviewed with. One of the main reasons she chose KPMG was because of what the Partner said at the final interview. He said, "We do not produce clones; we want everyone to keep and develop their own personality and individuality." He also told Alka that given she had travelled so far from Botswana, he wanted to let her know that KPMG would be making her an offer so that she would not have to wait another four to five weeks to get notification by letter as was the norm then.

The journey at KPMG wasn't easy; Alka was one of the very few interns from a foreign university. This was also the first time in her life as a young adult that she was living alone and that too in a vast new city, country, and continent. Furthermore, due to a recession in the UK, KPMG, like other big firms, were generally only keeping interns who passed their exams in the first attempt. Given the very low average pass rates, that put a lot of pressure on Alka.

Photo of Alka

The internship provided Alka with some incredible work experience; it also provided her with the opportunity to work across a broad spectrum of industries ranging from oil &

gas, media, manufacturing, and banking. She thrived under the able guidance of some amazing leaders and great work culture at KPMG. She completed her UK ACA exams within three years and decided to continue working and getting post-qualification work experience with KPMG in London for a further two years.

Having worked incredibly hard for her UK ACA qualification and as she was enjoying her finance roles, Alka dropped the idea of taking up an MBA offer from one of the top colleges in the US.

After five years at KPMG in London, given her strict visa restrictions, Alka had to look for a work opportunity outside the UK. She got an exciting chance to work in Bermuda within the Internal Audit and Treasury departments of the Bank of Bermuda, and she relocated there. After two years, she came back to London and joined Ernst & Young in their Business Risk Consulting group and then moved shortly into the Management Consulting group, focusing on the Investment Management sector. This covered outsourcing of middle/back-office functions, post-merger integration, investment fund reorganization and launches, middle/back-office system selection and implementation, and business process improvement.

All this while, Alka had an Indian passport and had stayed in these different countries either on work permits or on a child visa as a dependent of her parents. She didn't get permanent residency in Botswana due to her stay there as a dependent of expatriate parents. So, as she moved across countries and continents, she always felt the need to create a sense of belonging and a home wherever she was. Her management consultancy projects involved a lot of travel. Still, unlike her UK and European colleagues, it wasn't as easy for her to travel internationally for work due to onerous visa requirements. During the cross-border travel, her colleagues would pass and clear through immigration at the airport very quickly using the returning citizens' queue, whereas she would stand in a long queue of foreign passport holders, and her colleagues waiting at the other end were often surprised by this.

E&Y sponsored her UK residency, and after completing the required years of stay in the UK, she got UK Citizenship. India does not allow the holding of dual citizenship or passports so, surrendering her Indian passport was poignant and emotional; in her heart, it felt as if her roots were being cut off. It sure was a very tough decision, but she reminded herself that if she wanted to stay in the UK and travel easily with very few restrictions, then this was the best choice for her.

Having previously been her client at Ernst and Young in 2002, she was offered the role of Head of Operations – Hedge Fund and Private Equity by Schroders in London and was made responsible for setting this up. She had no prior experience in a line operations role and persisted and worked diligently to familiarize herself and get up to speed. She set up and built the team, operations, systems, and infrastructure in a cost-efficient, robust, and scalable manner. After three years in this role, the leadership made a strategic decision to outsource the middle and back-office operations for the entire business, including the hedge funds. Alka led the initiative to find, select and appoint a suitable outsourced service provider and to implement the outsourcing arrangement for the hedge funds. These were very challenging times but also one of great teamwork and leadership experience for her. It took over a year to implement the outsourcing, and she had to keep her team motivated when they knew that in the end, they would lose their jobs to the vendor. For those who wanted to stay at Schroders, Alka worked with HR and engaged directly with other parts of the business where she had built internal contacts to find them other suitable opportunities, and for those who wanted to find new jobs, she helped to negotiate a suitable redundancy package.

Alka then got the opportunity of a COO/CFO role with a smaller boutique Hedge Fund Investment management firm.

The Hedge Fund Industry has and continues to be a very male-dominated industry. Furthermore, the environment in a smaller firm is very different from that of the larger firms Alka had previously worked with. Partnership, collaboration, nimble decision making, and building trusted relationships with the Investment Manager and Capital Raising teams is critical to succeeding in such roles. Her team, client, service and relationship focus, perseverance, adaptability, and resilience helped her establish herself. The role is very broad and complex, and no one person can be an expert in all the areas, but by having an end-to-end understanding of all the different aspects of the business, Alka was able to find the right solutions, take on full responsibility for, and influence the decision making and direction of the business.

Whenever she attended the various Hedge Fund events and fora, there were few women and generally no more than 10-15 women COO/CFOs amongst the attendees. The question about this lack of women and diversity in the industry always popped in her mind, especially in the Investment and Senior Leadership roles. Over the next few years and as she had a family, Alka realized that the very demanding and long hours and the lack of cover at work have made it less attractive for women, and, this combined with the general lack of awareness of the potential opportunities has meant that there isn't a large pool or pipeline of available candidates either, so it will take time to address this issue.

Over the last four to five years, the investor community has begun focusing on diversity, which has heightened the awareness to hire more women, but there are no quick and easy solutions. It was only as recently as four years ago that "Women and Diversity and Inclusion" was selected as an agenda item for the first time in one of the annual hedge fund summits. A panel discussion was held on this topic and had four women and one male C-suite leader as panellists. During the discussion, the male leader shared how he had felt so nervous beforehand when he thought about being the only male amongst four highly talented and capable women leaders, and it dawned upon him how his women colleagues must feel every day working with a room full of mostly men.

On the personal front, Alka's parents being traditionally Indian, wanted her to get married in her early 20s after graduating from college in Botswana. They were very keen for her to continue her further education, but felt this could also be done after being married, and even tried to find a few men who they thought would be a suitable match for her. Alka was very clear in her mind that she did not want to get married until she had completed a professional qualification and begun working. While Alka worked in UK, Luxemburg, and Bermuda, her parents kept sharing profiles of Indian guys with her and eventually were very keen on her meeting a good partner and person from any background. Alka was in her 20s when two of her younger sisters got married, which was unusual for those times, but her parents and relatives joked that she had upheld an old family tradition of the eldest child getting married last. In her mid-thirties, Alka met Shiju in London through a common friend at a dinner party. Shiju is from Kerala; he grew up in India and Africa as well and was settled in the UK for many years. They got along very well and shared many core values.

After dating for four years, Shiju proposed, and they decided to get married a year later in Rajasthan, India. Though Shiju couldn't speak Hindi, a language spoken in Northern India and the only one understood by a lot of Alka's relatives, he was quick to engage with and make them all feel comfortable and at ease despite his language barrier.

Just before returning to London, the asset management company where Alka was working as the European COO/CFO, was taken over by Citigroup. Within a year of this merger,

Alka was pregnant and contemplating how many months of maternity leave she should take. The management team, which was mostly men, advised her to carry on working till one to two weeks before she was due and not take more than two months' leave. The head of HR however advised her to apply for a full year's leave and explained that, as it was the first child, she may not really know how long she may want to be off for, until after she had the baby. Moreover, if she wanted to come back sooner, she would always have the option to do that.

Alka and Shiju had a beautiful baby girl whom they named Avantika. Alka didn't instantly embrace motherhood; she felt a sense of loss of freedom, spontaneity, and control. She also had some baby blues and was also very overwhelmed and concerned that she didn't know or have any experience or understanding about bringing up and looking after the baby. It took her three months to feel confident and adjust to motherhood, after which she absolutely loved it. She decided to take a full year's maternity break as she was confident that on returning to work, she could hit the ground running even after a year off, given the stage of her career and 15 years of substantial professional experience behind her. Alka enormously appreciates that Shiju has given her space and fully supported her career. He has been a committed and very hands-on father to Avantika. This has been instrumental in allowing Alka to undertake the considerable demands and commitment required of her role.

She realized that going back to a boutique or startup Hedge Fund business would be very tough due to the long working hours and lack of cover. This was made harder with Shiju having to travel for work to India and South Asia at least 15 days of the month. Hence, she decided to return to a larger firm and joined JP Morgan Worldwide Securities Services (JPM WSS), London, as Head of Product Development for Global Pricing Operations. Though it was a London based role shortly after joining, Alka found she was having to travel and spend a lot of time away in the Edinburgh office, and so could not carry on with the role for one parent to be in London given also Shiju's work-related travel commitments.

She realized that it was difficult and challenging to manage a work-life balance even though she had the full support of her husband and a great nanny for her daughter. Given a young child and Shiju being away on work half of the time, Alka decided to work for a few years as an interim COO/CFO or on a project basis with a few select hedge funds and private equity clients. These assignments helped to keep her work experience current and relevant and to also manage her family commitments.

In 2015, she joined Onslow Capital Management Limited, a boutique Hedge Fund, as COO & CFO. Her journey there was both interesting and challenging, and she added value to the business and continued to learn a lot. Despite all the efforts to grow and expand the business, eventually, in early 2018, the leadership decided to return the existing investors their money and close the fund and business with Alka successfully leading an efficient and orderly wind-down.

During the COVID-19 crisis of 2020, Alka joined and supported TFA, a not-for-profit entity, as Finance Director. She provided strategic, financial, and commercial leadership to TFA and is a trusted adviser to the co-founders. This aligns with one of Alka's core values of always contributing to the community and to a social purpose. TFA was formed in April 2020 during the pandemic and so the team has successfully come together, worked and collaborated virtually and remotely. The business and leadership have had to constantly be fluid, navigate, and evolve in response to the extremely dynamic COVID situation. This is the first time Alka has been involved in the Healthcare industry, E-commerce business, and a not-for-profit organization. Her experience and resilience allowed her to pivot. When TFA was established, the expectation was that the COVID-19 situation would be under control in 12 months, and TFA would no longer be needed. TFA has launched 11 different COVID testing services and products and, for now, continues and is providing 75,000+ COVID Antibody tests and COVID PCR tests monthly.

Alka has worked hard, persevered, and taken the unique opportunities that have come her way to shape her own career while constantly adapting to the many changes in her life, from moving across continents to dealing with and learning to succeed in many varied and tough work environments. Changes in her life have been a constant and dealing with them hasn't always come to her naturally. She is committed to raising her daughter to be empathetic, confident, curious, comfortable with change, to be happy in her own skin and to work hard and persevere.

Alka's leadership mantras are:

- Lead by example.

- Be authentic and self-aware.

- Evolve and learn constantly.

- Have clarity of purpose and goals aligned with your customers, stakeholders, and team.

- Collaborate and build and manage strong relationships.

- Bring people along with you in the important decisions to be successful.

- Be flexible and adaptable.

- Voice yourself with confidence and articulate your thoughts well.

- Have a social purpose and community focus.

CHAPTER 9

Create Your Own Destiny

A girl born on the western coast of the Indian sub-continent in an educated family where women had voices and opinions in family matters grew up to become the CFO in a multinational company in India. She moved cities and countries to gain experience. She was always clear on what she wanted in life and dared to be clear about her expectations with people around her. Today, she is a doting grandmother and holding a senior executive position at a multinational company.

Rashmi Joshi was born in Dombivli, a small town in Thane district, Maharashtra, in India, in a middle-class Brahmin family. She is known for being a kind-hearted, self-driven, outspoken and very dependable woman. Education was important for her family, and she was always taught to be career-driven and independent. Her father was her role model since childhood. He was a dependable son in his family, and everyone looked up to him for advice.

When Rashmi was six years old, her parents decided that she would stay with her grandmother (Smt. Sushila Apte) for a year in her village. Rashmi loved staying with her grandmother where all her cousins visited every year. Her grandmother, whom she called Aaji, was an independent and capable lady. She managed the coconut farms, mango orchards, and paddy fields. Rashmi was fascinated as a child seeing her Aaji multitasking and managing the home and farms seamlessly. The farm workers would often interrupt Aaji while cooking to help them with any farm issues and Aaji would also offer solutions; Rashmi would sit beside her in the kitchen watching her cook and wonder how she could multitask? Rashmi would love to observe how Aaji used to manage the labour working on the farm, simultaneously going in and out of the kitchen and home. There were instances where the village people would come to Aaji with their health problems, and Aaji used to give them her special homemade natural remedies. Rashmi admired her Aaji's multitasking skills and the way she treated the labourers on the farms compassionately. Everyone in the village respected Aaji. She was a role model for her and continues so even today.

Honesty and integrity are the values that Rashmi picked up early on from Aaji. She was completely irked by dishonest and untruthful people from a very young age. Rashmi joined the village school for a year. In those days, kids in the village didn't have notebooks but carried a board made of stone (slate) on which they used to write with a white pencil. Her mother gave her a box of pencils, and her Aaji gave her one pencil every day while going to school. When she would return from school, her grandmother would check the school bag. On the days when the pencil was missing from the bag, Aaji would question Rashmi, "Where is the pencil I gave you this morning?" Rashmi would not lie and would tell that she gave it to someone in her class. She knew that some kids couldn't afford to buy the pencils, so she used to share with them. Aaji would smile back at her and would feel very proud of her.

When someone would visit Aaji's place, she would introduce Rashmi as a girl who is "one in a million," thanks to her being very bright in studies and generally well behaved. These words made a big impact on young Rashmi, and she was determined to live up to those expectations. As a child, she was very shy and yet very responsible. Her parents and family always felt proud of her. She was a very diligent kid and the favourite of all her teachers.

Photo of Rashmi and her family members

Life seemed just black or white for Rashmi as most folks in her family were straightforward and outspoken. She never realized there could be shades of grey until later when she joined the corporate world. She realized that people are different, not all would say what they mean, and non-verbal communication was as important as verbal, e.g., reading body language. Early in her career, Rashmi learnt the hard way that being outspoken is not always welcome. She then learnt to choose her words more carefully and wisely to convey her point of view cordially without compromising the truth.

She was fortunate to work for companies with the same values as her and was always encouraged to speak up if something was not right respectfully. As a CFO, one of the most important roles is to voice a concern if something is not right and support the organization in driving a culture of compliance. It is also imperative as a leader to create that environment in your team and company where everyone feels safe speaking up and sharing their opinions.

After spending a year in the village, Rashmi returned to live with her parents in a joint family. There was never a dedicated place for her to study, and she learnt how to focus and concentrate on her studies even in chaos. She loved music and languages like English, Marathi, and Hindi. She loved reading literature in these languages, and, as a child, believed that she would make a career in literature. Rashmi's father, Mr. Raghunath Thorat, was a Company Secretary (CS) and used to speak a lot about how the finance department was essential for any company. That led to Rashmi choosing commerce as a discipline for her graduation. While Rashmi was doing her graduation, her father asked her if she wanted to pursue Chartered Accountancy (CA) course one day. She discussed this option with her professor, whom she trusted. He also advised her to pursue a Chartered Accountancy course. This gave Rashmi confidence, and she applied for the course while pursuing graduation. Being away from the main city of Mumbai, she didn't have access to renowned firms, so she joined a local CA firm as an intern. Her life became hectic and the days were long with college studies, internship, and CA studies. One day Rashmi's mother, Mrs. Rekha Thorat, was worried about her daughter. She checked with Rashmi, "Why are you stretching yourself so much? Remember that even if you get a professional degree and job after marriage, you still have to manage household responsibilities along with the job!!" Rashmi laughed and responded that she would manage both and loved what she was doing. She cleared her CA exams and then enrolled on a Company Secretary course to get a complementary professional degree.

Rashmi qualified as a Chartered Accountant in the year 1988. In those times in India, it wasn't common for companies to hire women professionals. With no LinkedIn or online portals in those times, newspaper advertisements were the only medium to find a job if you didn't belong to an influential family. Every morning Rashmi would wake up early and read the newspaper, searching for jobs in Mumbai. She still remembers that many job advertisements specifically mentioned that only male candidates could apply. Months went by, and no luck. While Rashmi was employed in a CA firm, she dreamt of working for a big organization in the industry.

In many cases, she could not apply or was not selected because she was a woman who was unmarried and stayed outside the city. Employers refrained from investing their resources in training a girl who they believed would someday leave the job and get married or maybe could not work late hours being a woman. Rashmi was disheartened by the discrimination that she had to face in the job market. Finally, one day she came across an opportunity in Reliance. They were hiring a batch of women CAs. She applied for that job even though it was a long commute from her home. She was selected and hired.

Soon her parents found a match for her, and she got married to Satish. He, too, was a Chartered Accountant having a practice of his own. The marriage was a typical arranged marriage where Rashmi and Satish met and spoke only a few times before getting married. Rashmi had only one wish that she raised with Satish, she wanted to continue to pursue her career post marriage, and it sure was granted!!

Satish's family was well educated, and his mother was a working woman. Everyone in her family post marriage supported Rashmi in her career. Once she was blessed with a baby girl, it was difficult for her to manage the long commute time, and she looked for a job closer to her home. These were challenging times, and like any other working mother, Rashmi too struggled with a young daughter, household responsibilities, and a demanding work schedule. Especially on days when her daughter was sick, and Rashmi had to be at work, she would feel very guilty. Thanks to the support she had from her mother at the time, Rashmi had some relief.

In the year 1992, she joined a company at a managerial position in finance which gave her exposure to financial statement consolidation and management reporting. Most days were long with working weekends during the month-end. All this was possible because of the unconditional support of her family. Both her parents and in-laws supported her by taking care of her daughter and even helping her with school work. Rashmi's daughter Neeti was a responsible child, just like her mother. Neeti was very focused and methodical for her age. There were times when Rashmi would come back late from the office longing to spend time with her daughter but used to find her asleep or busy completing her homework. Rashmi did feel the guilt of not spending a lot of time with her daughter like some other mothers but was never worried as she was aware that her daughter was in safe hands.

It was very important for Rashmi that her daughter be well educated and follows her own path to make a career of her choice. Neeti went on to become an ACCA and CA and is working in finance function in a multinational organization. She is married and settled in Mumbai.

Rashmi had an aim to become the CFO of a company, but she knew that staying in a big corporate would take her longer to achieve this goal. Then came an opportunity of a Finance Director position for India Operations in a multinational company in the food industry which acquired a company in India. Rashmi's joining coincided with the company's global controllership meet in Jakarta. This was the first time she travelled outside India. When boarding the flight, Rashmi was very nervous, and multiple thoughts were running in her mind as no one in India knew about this organization, and she too did not know anyone in the

Photo of Rashmi

company. However, everything worked out fine. The global meet helped her establish connections in the company in the early days. She was exposed to the open and inclusive culture of the organization through various conversations she had with her colleagues. During dinners with her colleagues, Rashmi would always dress in the Indian traditional attire or sarees, and her colleagues were in awe of the vibrant colours and the elegance of the attire and could not stop asking more about it. She was warmly welcomed into the team and was made to feel included right from day one. After returning to India, the work on setting up the India operations for the company began. Apart from finance, Rashmi managed the administration and technology set-up as well. It was great learning and exposure for her. She thoroughly enjoyed her work and was glad that it also allowed her to strike a great work-life balance.

After the 9/11 incidence when global markets crashed, the company decided to shut down its India set-up. She was given a year's notice by the company to help wind up operations. It was a difficult phase for Rashmi as she was aware of the decision while many others were not. She had to often control her emotions in front of other colleagues to ensure not letting out anything. In due course, the management communicated the decision to the employees. Many of those impacted had a challenging time absorbing the news. She remembers a support staff breaking down in Rashmi's presence and saying that he did not have enough savings even to feed his family for a month. Rashmi never felt more helpless. She, however, made sure that he was placed in another organization soon. After a few days when she received a call from him, thanking her and explaining how happy he was at this new place, Rashmi felt satisfied.

During this time, Rashmi did her best to support the team members to find opportunities and started looking for a new opportunity herself. She realized how important it is for an institution to survive and thrive as many people survive and thrive with it. It is the responsibility of the leadership to ensure that business operations continue and contribute to society by providing livelihood and career opportunities.

That time, Rashmi was clear that her next stint would be in a bigger organization. She then landed an opportunity as a finance controller in the white goods industry, but the position was based out of Gurugram in Northern India. Rashmi was happy about the profile, and she was sure that the experience would set her up for success in the future. When she first informed her friends and family, their first reaction was, "Nobody goes for finance profiles from Mumbai to Gurugram as Mumbai is the financial hub of India." However, her husband Satish told her that if she thinks this opportunity is the right career move for her, she must go for it. These words by Satish boosted Rashmi's confidence in her decision which wasn't easy. She enjoyed her stay in Gurugram for two years with her daughter and family coming in from time to time. But Mumbai remained home, and it became clear that she would move back to Mumbai once she gets a great opportunity.

In the year 2005, Rashmi got an opportunity as General Manager Finance at Castrol India in Mumbai. Rashmi was back in Mumbai with her daughter, and life seemed to settle for her. She was enjoying her profile and, within three years, was promoted to a senior position, but her role changed due to a restructuring in the company. She was offered two options by her company; one role was based in India and another in Singapore as Regional Performance Manager. Rashmi chose the latter as she believed that it would add international exposure to her career journey. It was also the perfect timing as her daughter had completed her high school, and so she could enrol in a graduation course in Singapore. This time also Rashmi relocated to Singapore with her daughter, and Satish decided to stay back in Mumbai for his work. After one year and a half, Satish decided to quit his employment in Mumbai and join his family in Singapore. All the relatives and friends gave a shocked reaction to this news as it wasn't common in India to be a trailing spouse. Satish and Rashmi were very clear that they wanted to live together as a family in one place and supported each other in this decision.

By then, Rashmi had completed almost four years in Singapore. During that time, her father's health deteriorated, and her mother was unable to deal with it alone. Rashmi's siblings had also settled away from home, and there was no family support available. Satish and Rashmi then decided that, given the circumstances, they should move back to India to take care of their parents. Rashmi requested the senior management for a role back in India. The management was kind to consider the request favourably. Coincidentally, the Castrol India CFO position opened, and she successfully competed to get the role. Rashmi is grateful to Castrol India and its parent company British Petroleum Group (BP) for the support and care she received from her leaders and colleagues and the opportunities she got there to progress.

Rashmi, as a caring daughter, not only supported her parents but also established herself as one of the most respected woman CFO leaders in India. She received numerous prestigious awards, Best Woman CFO award by Business World India in the year 2016, the CFO of the year 2018 Award by Financial Express, and The Asia Woman Adam Smith Awards2019 by Treasury Today Publications. In seven years, she was able to take the finance team to the next level of performance with her progressive thinking and change agility. She also translated efficiency targets into an opportunity for digital evolution keeping the team energized for the major change. According to her, "The most important role of a CFO is to protect the interests of all stakeholders of the company. CFO needs to know the art of storytelling in business events and weave numbers into the same story. The CFO needs to keep everyone in the company focused on their targets and performance through very transparent reporting and at the same time co-create solutions with the team to meet those targets." As a leader, being a team player is essential towards taking everyone along the journey to achieve a common vision. As you climb up the corporate ladder, it is even more important to influence and collaborate.

The year 2020 with the pandemic was one of the most difficult years on the personal front for Rashmi. Her mother was at the last stages of dementia when the lockdown was announced by the Indian Government. Rashmi became a grandmother in the same year when her daughter became a mother to a lovely boy. Managing work, home, mother's health, and daughter with a young child, at the same time without domestic help due to the pandemic was getting overwhelming for her.

However, Rashmi is grateful for the experience of being a proud and doting grandmother to Pradyut—a handsome and healthy boy. It is a 'money cannot buy' experience and like none other in the world for her.

Around the same time, Rashmi's organization announced a large scale restructuring which meant uncertainty of jobs for everyone in the organization. Rashmi decided to treat this as an opportunity instead of adversity and got into another role that was global in nature that had a larger team and broader responsibility. However, she had to go through a rigorous selection process to land the role and had to wait for a few months to know the result of the process. Rashmi has recently moved into a new role of Head of General Accounting & Assurance for Global Business Services Centre of BP plc based in Pune, leading a large global general accounting team with digitization, standardization, and transformation as key agenda. Rashmi is also leading a business resource group, bpWIN, in the Pune Centre to drive more diversity, equity, and inclusion for women.

On September 9, 2020, Rashmi lost her mother. It was a very traumatic experience for her. None of her relatives could visit her due to the lockdown. She had to do the last rites for her mother with help from her husband and neighbours. Times were hard, but her grandson was a pleasant distraction from her sorrow, and she found solace in looking after him and her work.

After her daughter went back to her own home, Rashmi and her husband decided to focus on the completion of their farmhouse at her father's hometown close to Alibag near Mumbai. Focusing on the project, dealing with the challenges of building something in a small village kept Rashmi busy, and she enjoyed the creative process. Being close to nature also helped her heal.

Throughout her career, Rashmi has been sincere, authentic, adaptable, and that helped her succeed and grow. She has taken calculated risks to rise in her career and to gain diverse experience. The journey wasn't smooth, and there were professional and personal challenges, but she stayed firm, remembering the words of her Aaji, "Don't quit in difficult circumstances, fight back and come out stronger." The women in her life and family and her father provided her inspiration and support each day.

Rashmi's leadership mantras are:

- Be Authentic.
- Speak up.
- Genuinely care for others.
- Make your people (Team members, family members, friends) part of your vision.
- Create your own destiny.

CHAPTER 10

Handle the Crisis with a Positive Attitude

This young, soft-spoken girl was passionate about making a career in finance since her high school days. She navigated her way to the position of CFO after doing diverse finance roles across product costing, financial planning, controllership, treasury, and strategy and gaining experience across diverse industries and sectors.

Alessandra Segatelli was born in São Caetano do Sul, São Paulo state in Brazil. It was an industrial town with many automobile companies' production units. Her grandparents were immigrants from Italy and were settled in Brazil after World War II. Her father had 13 siblings, and they made a living by working on farms. He couldn't complete his studies as he had to focus on earning a living. Life was particularly tough for him, and he never really enjoyed his life. After marriage, he moved from the farms' area to São Caetano do Sul to work in a factory and earn more money. Alessandra and her brother Vanderlei had an ordinary childhood, but they both enjoyed each other's company. Their father enforced upon them each day the importance of education and wanted them to live a prosperous life when they grew up. They studied in a public school as their parents couldn't afford a private school. Alessandra's mother was a homeworker and had to quit her job after her marriage and kids. She always encouraged Alessandra to be financially independent and gave her a dream to study for a professional degree. She would tell her,

"I don't want you to live a life of a homemaker, I want you to live a life where you work even after marriage." As a child, her dream was to be an astronomer. As she did not have much access to technology, she enjoyed going to the library every week hunting for her favourite stars and planets and loved watching a TV Show called Cosmos by Carl Sagan.

Vanderlei was 18 months older than Alessandra, and they both played and fought like any other siblings. Most of the time after school was spent with neighbourhood kids playing a game of "Peteca", a Portuguese game like cricket, on the street. She liked to play with dolls with her friends at a young age but enjoyed the boy's games in the field more. When her brother would go out to play football with his friends, she would cry to take her along. Her mother would often instruct him to take her along and not make her cry. The poor boy felt so embarrassed taking his sister along but had no option. They both had a passion for collecting T cards which continues to date. After high school, Vanderlei joined a university professional course to become a doctor. Their father being a worker in a factory, could fund university fees only for one of them. Alessandra was aware of the circumstances and decided to work along with her studies to fund her studies post-high school. She would come back from work tired, and on some days, she didn't even feel like studying. In those moments, her mother would sit next to her and motivate her. She would tell her, "Don't give up now, these are tough times, but if you get a professional degree, then your life will be very different." She would keep reinforcing options available on how to concentrate and focus on studies along with work. There was a point in time when Vanderlei decided to leave his medical course midway as he wasn't enjoying it, considering that the medical course journey is long. At that time, his mother motivated him not to give up studies but rather imagine the feeling that he would be the first doctor in the entire family one day. And today, he is a successful Physician in one of the best hospitals in Brazil.

**Photo of Alessandra (middle) with her son and husband
(extreme right)**

Alessandra's first job was as a cost accountant in one of the manufacturing companies in her town. She was fortunate to work under a great leader who always made sure that his team members understood the end-to-end production process behind the numbers they work on. On the very second day of joining the organization, her leader took her along to the production floor to observe the process. As she entered the production floor where the heat treatment of raw material was taking place to convert it into gear and bearings, she observed that it was scorching, and workers were sweating. Each worker would work for an hour and then take 30 minutes break to cool himself down. Looking at the condition of the workers, she was reminded of her father; she could realize how her father worked in such a difficult environment to earn money for the family. That night she went back home and hugged her father tight, tears rolled down her eyes, and she said to him, "Thanks, for all that you do for us each day." He was touched by this gesture and cried with her.

Alessandra went to the manufacturing plant every day and learnt every step involved in the production line, which made her work as a cost accountant interesting and gave numbers a lot more meaning. During those times, very few females took up cost accounting jobs, and when visiting manufacturing plants, she learnt that her choice of dressing was important to not call for much attention. She would wear full sleeved shirts and trousers most of the time. Her boss was a German expat and treated males and females in his team equally.

She completed her graduation in Business Administration from the University of São Paulo. She joined as a qualified cost accountant in the beverages segment in the finance team in PepsiCo in the year 1992. This stint helped her gain experience in customer behaviour which is different in every market. Her team worked on costing for the launch of artificially flavoured fruit juice in Brazil; this product was one of the most profitable beverages in the US market for PepsiCo. The company invested in this product for launch in Brazil, and after monitoring two years of sales performance, the team realized that sales weren't picking up. When they deep dived further, they understood that customers in Brazil preferred natural fruit juice rather than a flavoured beverage. It made them realize that customer behaviour differs in each geography.

From the year 2005 to 2008, she moved into a Controllership role in Walt Disney. The work culture at Walt Disney was amazing, with a great focus on customer experience. All of the employees would watch the movie together before it was released in theatres. After watching the movie, they would express their opinion on the chances of success of that movie which would be the basis of financial forecast. When Alessandra joined the finance team at Walt Disney, the forecast for theatre movies revenue was based on review comments from employees after movie preview. She soon realized that assumptions were made based on emotions in this process. She then worked with regional finance teams to create power regression analysis-based forecasts backed by data. Revenue forecasts for each movie based on a theme were now made based on comparing the recent success of similar themes and target audience preferences data. The forecasting process based on emotions was replaced with data analytics.

Alessandra always believed in continuous learning, so in 2015, she decided to study Taxation further as she didn't have much experience in this subject. She studied Master of Science in Finance while working as Director at Herbalife. Before that, she completed the MBA in Economy while working as Business Controller at Danone.

Her husband was a constant support during all these times, which helped her focus on studies along with her career. She always felt that her husband, Silvio, had more belief in her when she had lost hope for herself. This helped her stay focused even in the difficult phases of her career.

She believes that in the Latin America region, which is a sexist society, it is very important for any career-oriented female to have the right partner who is supportive. She has always acknowledged the support of her partner, "My husband has always shared responsibilities of home and our son. He had been very supportive of my career all throughout my journey." As per a study, in Latin America, only 20% of females make it to a senior management position, and the C-suite positions are even harder for females. Alessandra has often attended finance events in Brazil, where the number of women leaders is as low as only 8 women in a room of about 100 people. In 2020, Alessandra, along with other seven women CFOs in Brazil, founded the W-CFO group to mentor young female professionals. Today, they have over 50 females enrolled for mentoring sessions. She thinks that '*A woman usually applies for a job only when she thinks she is 100% ready vs. a man who would apply for a job only when 75% ready.*'

Alessandra is determined to bring about a change in this attitude amongst young female professionals. She mentors them and grooms them to change this mindset and be more confident.

After being a mom, Alessandra wisely began segregating urgent vs. important. Silvio and Alessandra always made sure that their only son, Guilherme Yudi Segatelli Tanabe understands the importance of family. Both her husband and she ensured that they spent quality time with him, helping him complete the homework, playing games, and reading books. They had Vera and Rita as nanny and house help who helped them raise him. There were times when the nanny would take him to dentists or after school extracurricular classes. The young boy would often visit his grandfather and would spend evenings playing with him and help him with dinner. Alessandra feels lucky that she had a supportive ecosystem at home that ensured the great upbringing of Guilherme and allowed her to focus on office work.

Today, their son is a grown-up boy applying for admissions in universities, and they are helping him choose a course of his choice and motivating him. She would never forget when once her son was just a year old and her company wanted her to move to another role overseas. She had to say "No" to that opportunity given family priorities, and her manager gave her feedback that she can never become CFO unless she takes up diverse roles. She took this feedback seriously and made a conscious choice to move to diverse roles in finance across different companies in São Paulo. Alessandra was successfully making career moves with this strategy, but then came a time when she took up a controllership role in one company. But due to organizational restructuring, she was asked to move back to (Financial Planning & Analysis) FP&A role. She bravely accepted that role even though it wasn't aligned to her career plan, but it turned out to be a lucky move as she got the opportunity to work on a critical strategic project within the FP&A team.

Photo of Alessandra

She started her career with finance for the supply chain and moved to be a finance business partner for the commercial pricing and marketing areas. After this experience, she had the chance to take up controllership, completing her knowledge of finance roles. With her continuous perseverance and having a great team by her side, she earned multiple awards during her career.

Her team at Herbalife earned the award for the best forecast accuracy in the organization. Her team also won a prize from Treasury Today magazine, in the United Kingdom, with the best card solution for customers. She recalls that she filled up the competition form for this Treasury award without much hope of winning it. When the results were announced through an email, she and her partner Juliana were super thrilled and happy. Both of them were invited to London for the award ceremony night. Everyone in the family was really excited for her. She and Juliana spent time together on a week-long trip and became good friends for a lifetime. Both also got an opportunity to attend a musical concert at the Wimbledon stadium. When Alessandra entered the stadium, she just couldn't believe that she was at Wimbledon; tears of happiness rolled down her cheeks. The award news made her and Juliana famous in their organization. It was the first time ever that a Latin America-based team had received this prestigious award.

In the year 2017, she got an opportunity as CFO for the Latin America region Pearson Ltd, a company in Education Industry. Moving to the CFO role, Alessandra pivoted her leadership style to provide guidance to the team, interact more with team members and other stakeholders, partner with business heads and CEOs to provide solutions. She focused on building a solid team to enable her to free up her time and effort towards strategic decision making for the company.

As a successful CFO, she believes it is imperative to focus on strategic demands from a business partner and, at the same time, provide good support to the team. Leading is about inspiring and changing the mindset instead of just delegating. Over the years, the CFO role has evolved even more to that of a business partner, which meant understanding the business in detail, being curious about products and services offered and at the same time being aware of external perspectives. One of the challenges her treasury team was facing was how to equip the commercial sales team with data about the financial condition of prospective clients. Since this data wasn't readily available, the sales team was struggling to expand the customer base. Alessandra and the team worked hard in creating a database for financial information of all corporates in the region by hiring an external vendor for real-time information update in the database. The finance team then worked with the technologies team to create a Mobile App through which the sales team could fetch the required data on the field. This information helped the sales team to negotiate with clients and onboard financially sound clients.

The year 2020 provided yet another learning opportunity to Alessandra. The year that was hit hard by the global pandemic crisis and was probably the toughest year for most businesses in a long time… She worked with business partners to create a plan on daily cashflows, daily Accounts Receivable positions and created innovative business solutions to help the customers and students. Being in the education industry, the team pivoted quickly to move to 100% digital content for patrons. They partnered with insurance companies to provide insurance cover to students so that they could continue with their studies. As CFO of the company, she worked as a team with business heads to provide new solutions in commercial space to help the company sail through the crisis.

Latin America region has faced and survived an economic crisis without a strong infrastructure and education system. Being born in this region, handling crises and problem solving came naturally to Alessandra. She faced many challenging periods during her career as a result of this economic environment ranging from working for companies struggling to survive, restructuring, harsh takeovers and managing adverse reactions of the investors. During all these challenging phases as a finance professional, she remained positive and partnered with business heads and senior management to find a solution. During her professional journey, on the one hand, she worked with great leaders, and on the other hand, she has experienced difficult situations such as fraud, and compliance issues which were stressful. She can never forget the day when she reported a fraud event she had identified after a deep investigation to her CEO. To her surprise, she was requested to not report it to the global headquarters. She could not sleep that night, and the next day she told the CEO that she would be reporting the event to the global team and she would love to have him on the call. She told him that even though he had suggested otherwise, she felt it was her duty to report the event, and he must be the first person to know about her decision. At the end of the day, he participated in the meeting, mentioning he was the one who decided to bring everyone together and call their attention to the fraud event. After this instance, she decided to leave the company as she didn't want to work for a boss who did not act with integrity. Alessandra recalls, "Every professional would have situations in career when they might be tempted to cross the line outside their own core values. Whenever faced with such situations, find the courage to stand for your values and make decisions in the best interests of the organization."

Alessandra's leadership mantras are:

- Be kind to yourself. You don't have to be perfect always.

- Listen to people around you. Solutions often come by working together.

- You will be remembered as a leader from how you treat someone.

- Take care of your spiritual side apart from your mind and body.

CHAPTER 11

Finding the Hero within You

This is the story of the granddaughter of a Buddhist monk who made a name in the finance field through her hard work and determination. She funded her education, volunteered to take up difficult assignments, and took informed risks to grow in her career. Sonam Donkar made it to the CFO position at a very young age. She is the only female CFO in the mining industry in India. Her hard work, resilience, collaboration skills, and ability to take risks helped her in this journey.

Sonam's grandfather, Bhato Bhutia, has had a great influence on her. Bhato was from Lhasa, Tibet. Born in a rich business family and being the eldest son, he was sent to the monastery to become a monk. Like every eldest child (son) in a Tibetan household, he was sent to a monastery at an early age. He had to give up his life's comforts and become a monk undergoing strict laws of detachment, sacrifice, and compassionate living. In his 20s, around the year 1935, he, along with a few other senior monks, decided to travel to India to visit the Bodhi tree under which Lord Buddha achieved *nirvana*. The destiny had something else in store for him. When the group was crossing the Tibet–India border, they were detained by the British Army as they misunderstood them as Chinese infiltrators. They were detained in prison for a few weeks, but when they explained that they were monks from Tibet and not from China, the British Army offered them an option to be foot soldiers in the British Indian Army if they wanted to stay alive. The entire group of monks joined the army to save their lives. Bhato was the smartest and the bravest of them all and was soon elevated to senior ranks. Once India got independence in the year 1947, Bhato joined the Tibetan Self Help Centre in India to help Tibetans who were taking refuge in India. He helped establish vocational training facilities for refugees and wrote articles on this topic in Indian newspapers.

Sonam, as a child, loved spending time with Bhato. He told her stories of bravery and heroism. He always mentioned to Sonam, "Anyone can be a hero; you have to find what makes you a hero." This has stuck with her, and since her childhood, Sonam keeps searching for that heroism in herself each day.

Sonam's parents Topgyal and Palmo, lived in a small town near Darjeeling and had a very modest background. They decided to move to Delhi to give their children the opportunity of studying at some of the best schools/colleges in India. Sonam grew up in Delhi, but finding space for herself to study in a 9X9 square foot one-room home where a family of five would live together wasn't easy. She would sometimes study in the bathroom to get that space for herself. Since childhood, she aspired to get a well-paid job and a stable economic life after completing her education. Though she couldn't afford a lavish lifestyle in her childhood, her parents and school taught her to give back to the community by helping others with whatever resources one has. Being from a Buddhist family, since early days, Sonam used to walk with her parents to the monastery to donate food as offerings. Additionally, Sonam's school had special sessions for educating the helpers of the school and kids from nearby slum areas for which students could volunteer. This environment at home and school inculcated a strong habit of paying it forward to communities in her.

Sonam was always a hardworking student and continued to focus on learning and how to be financially independent. After completing high school, she made it to Shri Ram College

**Photo of Sonam as teenager (extreme left) with her parents
and brother**

of Commerce in Delhi University, the top college in India for Commerce studies. However, she decided to forego a formal commerce degree and instead joined Bachelor's in Business Studies course from Delhi University so that she could earn as an industrial trainee while studying and get a job after graduation. After completing this course, she applied to the course for a Master's in Finance from Delhi University. This was after her dream for an MBA had broken with the Common Entrance Test (CAT) paper being leaked in India that year.

Sonam got placed as a management trainee with Ballarpur Industries in the Corporate Finance team and was lucky to find a great mentor, Sudhir Mathur, who was back then the CFO of that company. He was around 37 years old, a humble, well-read, and smart leader who brought value to the company in multiple ways. Sonam was the only female in that finance team, and in three years, she created space for herself by stepping up and volunteering for difficult projects. Sudhir always made sure that her opinions and thoughts were heard even though she was a trainee on the project. This helped Sonam to be confident, and she didn't hesitate to share her thoughts in the presence of senior leaders. Sonam also got an opportunity to shadow Sudhir on some projects, which helped her gain firsthand experience of how a CFO thinks, manages his day, and prioritizes tasks.

Sudhir motivated Sonam to work on her MBA dream. She decided to give MBA one more shot in the year 2005 and she finally managed to crack the entrance test.

Sonam began her MBA programme at IIM Bangalore and got placed with Standard Chartered Bank in Delhi in the financial markets profile on the completion of her course. In 2007 during the mortgage crisis, all banks started reviewing their practices to ensure risk management. For instance, one of the practices was that the sales teams were given steep targets with huge rewards linked to them. If the team were given a $4 million sales target, their incentives were computed as a certain % of their sales. To meet these targets, the sales teams resorted to instant profit-making ideas which were not always in the best interests of the customers. Sonam, during that period, worked on win-win strategies for both the customers and the bank, enabling successful long-term customer partnerships. Working in a banking environment chasing targets, Sonam realized that she wanted to create a greater impact and do more than just manage accounts. Her desire to create long-term value for business was much stronger than what a lucrative high-paying banking career could offer.

After three years, she joined Dell, Bangalore, as a Treasury Controller. The profile provided her with international exposure with a multi-cultural team. She also managed one of the key mergers & acquisitions events. While all this brought great learnings, one question Sonam would ask herself often was, "Am I using my full potential?" Sonam felt the role wasn't giving her the opportunity to demonstrate an entrepreneurial mindset.

Indra Nooyi, CEO of PepsiCo, was one of the role models for Sonam. She always followed her speeches and her interviews available on online platforms. One afternoon, she got a call from a headhunter for a job opportunity at PepsiCo. Sonam just jumped from her chair with excitement, given the fact that if she could get a role at PepsiCo, she would get to hear her role model more often. Sonam joined PepsiCo India as Head of Treasury & Controller of Commercial Exports. This role as a "Mini CFO" of a small division sowed a seed of inspiration in Sonam to aspire for a more extensive CFO profile in the future. With supportive mentors like Mr. Deepak Kini and Mr. Chetan Mathur and women leaders Indra Nooyi and India CFO, Kimsuka Narsimhan to look up to, it was indeed a career transforming journey. Sonam never hesitated to take on more and more challenging roles at PepsiCo and kept raising her performance bar. Her career moves at Pepsi were not shortsighted for promotions but rather for adding diverse experiences to her resume.

Sonam led critical assignments in Pepsi; she worked on rural entry strategy, empowering rural women to set up shops for beverages/snacks and deploy coolers through financing support from MSME financiers. She worked closely with business teams managing the logistics and financing for making it happen with a critical launch during the summer months in key markets in India. Sonam was pregnant during that time, but she passionately led this project as she felt that it was not just about selling the products but also empowering women entrepreneurs to build their livelihood. During the pregnancy period, while Sonam had long working hours at the office, she had great support from her colleagues, including male team members. Many times, her colleagues would volunteer to stay back late in the office to offload work from Sonam so that she could leave on time. They would also get healthy snacks for her.

In the year 2014, Sonam was blessed with a baby boy. While being a mother, she felt blessed, but she also realized that she needed to plan for everything and prioritize her tasks. Being at home when the baby was mostly sleeping, she kept herself busy by planning for her retirement funds, and she made investment decisions with a long-term view. She also started practising yoga during this time which was immensely beneficial and has become an essential part of her life. Sonam also started planning what support system she needed to create for her baby when she joined back work. She monitored the time and effort required for each activity to take care of the baby in her absence and then hired additional help at home who could manage that work in her absence. She moved to breast pumps to graduate from breastfeeding to bottle feeding. Many in her own family raised their eyebrows when she discussed her return to work. There were questions and comments like "How can you think of leaving behind a three-month-old baby?" "Why can't you take a career break?" But Sonam's husband, Tenzing Namdhak, was very supportive; Tenzing assured Sonam that she could join back work and everything would get managed. Also, Sonam's mother kept encouraging her to pursue dreams

Photo of Sonam

that she couldn't do as a homemaker. After three months of maternity break, she joined back since she knew that a few critical assignments that she had started before she went on maternity leave needed some finishing touches.

It was in the year 2017, during a conversation with one of her mentors, that he mentioned to her that doing diverse roles would help her grow as a stronger finance professional. He quoted the example of Bollywood turned Hollywood star Priyanka Chopra who is known for multi-faceted skills as an actor, singer, producer, etc. This changed her mindset and led her to experiment more and broaden her exposure taking up challenging roles within finance, partnering closely with business at the grass-roots level. In her last year at PepsiCo, Sonam took up the role of Commercial Finance Strategy. She travelled to different cities in India and Kirana stores to understand the grass-root level distribution systems. She worked on creating strategies that made the overall discount system more effective in all distribution channels. She also led the Commercial finance and sales strategy across all channels. To build a robust sales price discount strategy and build a corrective plan on potential leakages, she visited 100+ key retail outlets in the biggest markets in India. She gathered feedback by interacting with key outlets as well as engaging with distributors mapped to those markets. Basis these continuous market visits, the team could build deep insights around product pricing gaps vis a vis competition and inefficiencies in supply order management due to manual order booking. This led to the genesis of the Zero Touch Program that involved transparent information sharing, order booking through mobile devices with real-time inventory mapping and information tracking.

During her career, Sonam did a short stint at Unilever, where she also got the opportunity to work in the operations department. She was tasked to improve the overall efficiency in supply chain management for a Lakme Product line. The product was high margin and low volume play, so it was critical to have highly efficient order management in line with the production plan. For a detailed understanding of the processes and issues at the grass-root level, she visited key third-party manufacturers and their vendors across Gujarat and Mumbai. She mapped overall issues and levels of manual intervention needed at each step. With the help of detailed insights, she was able to build process flows and a model to help plan overall inventory and production. This scientific analysis helped quantify and improve overall efficiency, mapping qualitative and quantitative issues across the value chain and strengthening the overall sales and operations planning.

Working in PepsiCo, Sonam was always inspired by Indra Nooyi, who would spend time with women leaders in India during her visits to India. Indra always showed reality to everyone that professional life is not a bed of roses, but one needs to work hard to achieve professional goals. A female must always prove herself more than a male counterpart, and even if you get a position because of the diversity goals of the organization, you can't afford to underperform. Tough choices will have to be made each day.

In the year 2018, an opportunity for a CFO role knocked on Sonam's door. She joined Vedanta Group as their CFO Commercial Organization. It was a leap from FMCG Industry to Metal Mining Industry, and Sonam was given a steep goal of value addition to the company's bottom line of approx. $2 billion. Sonam took the bull by the horns and acquired an in-depth understanding of the metal mining industry. She then worked on setting up a new team and guided it successfully with her determination and perseverance. Vedanta's leadership team gave her the empowerment and independence to operate, and within 18 months, her role was expanded as CEO for the group's asset monetization.

Her professional aspirations were further catapulted by direct mentoring from the promoters as well as the Chairman and Vice-Chairman of Vedanta as they personally invested time in creating a healthy culture of diversity in the company. The philosophy was further harboured via a strong support system of other senior leaders who ensured the success of each young leader in the company. The fact that a woman could have a seat and voice at the table inspired many women managers to grow at Vedanta. Sonam's growth story, along with other growth stories within the group, has been constantly highlighted, and a mentor-mentee programme has been set up at Vedanta to ensure the right coaching for young women managers.

Within six months of joining Vedanta, Sonam was selected for the Chairman's high-profile taskforce projects and given additional responsibility. She was also nominated to be part of many senior-level committees to drive key agendas of digitization, outsourcing, and integration of Commercial and Marketing functions, which involved field visits, expert engagement, and implementation. Further, she was offered multiple senior-level opportunities to lead Group Commercial functions, and lead a promising business as Unit lead and CFO of the largest metal mining firm. Such elevation and encouragement to women leaders across the level is one of its kind and has increased commitment and passion for delivering more across the ranks in the company.

2020—a year of multiple challenges turned out to be a year of opportunities for Vedanta and Sonam as she took on the role of CFO of one of the largest businesses of Vedanta. Under her leadership, the team flourished and performed their best. She continued engaging with front-line teams, workers at units, and peers through virtual mode, 24x7. During the COVID-19 nationwide lockdown in India, the mining activities were exempted. While on the business numbers side, there was no impact, the management had more responsibilities towards the emotional and physical wellbeing of front-line workers. Sonam pivoted her leadership style and made sure she had virtual connections with staff members across sites and dealt with them with more compassion. As soon as the lockdown was lifted, she travelled to each site to meet the staff in person, re-align on targets, reinvigorate, and challenge the targets with close dialogue and brainstorming sessions. In her view, timely rewarding and recognizing the winners has always made a difference, and sharing credit with the team is more important than standing out as a lone warrior.

During these times, Sonam spent almost 90% of her time connecting with folks at all levels in the organization and understanding the human side of professionals. She travelled across cities at the mining sites meeting the front-line managers, listening to them, and addressing their problem areas and concerns. Focus on business as well as rewarding and acknowledging the teams working round the clock during lockdown was more critical and has thus resulted in exemplary business numbers with the best performance for the Aluminium & Power Business that Sonam is responsible for.

During the second COVID wave in India in April 2021, many of her staff members (immediate and at the factory) were impacted by COVID-19, and at the same time, she lost some family members too. It was emotionally a very challenging phase for Sonam. On the one hand, she had to manage the family front, and on the other, she had to ensure that the employees at work are motivated and have her support. As the second wave of COVID was peaking, Sonam made sure that she was personally in touch with mining workers across India. She travelled by air during this time, risking her life. Every time she planned an official trip, she had to get an RTPCR test to ensure that she is COVID-19 negative. In this process, she built great relationships with employees and motivated young women trainees to aspire for higher roles. During the interactions with the employees, she made sure that apart from work status, she would check on the physical and mental status of each one of them.

Sonam's husband, Tenzing Namdhak, and both their parents have been the backbone supporting her in managing the work-life priorities to balance long working hours. Her secret to multitasking lies in extremely meticulous planning, bucketing professional commitments and personal commitments based on priority, and balancing it all on a tight rope.

As a woman leader, Sonam continues to invest time in grooming women talent in her team and mentors young women managers in India. Additionally, she also mentors and spends time with NGOs that focus primarily on the education sector. In her words, she works extra hard each day to carve out space and time for the perfect balancing act!!

Sonam's leadership mantras are:

- Stay humble and honest.

- It's important to lead but even more important to be a great team player.

- Encourage young leaders and women professionals; a soft push can work magic for them.

- There is no substitute for hard work, so keep walking.

Made in the USA
Coppell, TX
15 December 2022

89476306R00079